Fire Island Taxi Driver

*Recollections of Summers on
the Beach at Fabulous Fire Island, NY
1960–64*

PETER CHRISTIAN OLSEN

LUCAS PARK

BOOKS

ST. LOUIS, MISSOURI

Cover photo of Fire Island postcard used with the permission of Found Image Press Inc. (foundimage.com)

Cover photo of Fire Island taxi used with permission of:

>Mr. Eric Olsen

>Mr. and Mrs. Edwin & Susan Olsen

ACKNOWLEDGMENTS
The author wishes to acknowledge the following people without whose editorial assistance, this manuscript might never have seen the light of day. Mr. Frank Kavanagh for scrupulous editorial assistance of every sentence in the book. Mrs. Barbara Trinkle whose helpful ideas and patient review allowed for a finished project.

Some of the names of people in the story have been modified to protect their anonymity.

Print ISBN: 978-1-60350-046-3

Published by Lucas Park books
www.lucasparkbooks.com

Printed in the United States of America

Contents

Introduction

It was hard to imagine any red-blooded American college coed thinking about anything less than summer in the sun during school vacation. As May faded into June, that was all I thought about. And yet being a semi-responsible soon-to-be-adult, I wanted to alleviate my parents from further financial burdens by earning some cash to help defray those college expenses, like tuition, books, and beer. I had to work during summer vacation. But sometimes the stars line up perfectly and the gods shine their light on you. I inherited fabulous good luck. I managed to combine these two objectives in a way that felt almost transcendent. I found a summer job that paid exceedingly well and proved to be most pleasant and gratifying; that is to say there was lots of cash and plenty of fun in the sun.

Some back story here helps to set the stage for this phenomenal good luck. About 1956, two brothers-in-law who frequented the beach at Fire Island, NY recognized that no reliable transportation was available to the summer residents. Fire Island, a well-known resort inhabited summers by a large clientele from the New York area is essentially a barrier island five miles off the south coast of Long Island. No roads exist on the island and transportation is solely along the beach front. Scattered some distance apart are a diversity of eclectic communities each distinct in attitude, culture, and population. Residents expressed a desire to move about between the communities but were unwilling to trudge long distances through soft sand in the hot sun.

Enter the two brother's-in-law with their innovation— White Cap Taxi Service. With an aging fleet of dilapidated four-wheel-drive Willys jeeps, often held together with bailing wire, duct tape, and an assortment of nuts and bolts, they began their transportation service. The idea spread like wild fire and their clientele blossomed. It was a summer only

1

enterprise. As the phenomenon grew, they needed drivers to keep up with the demand. I was ready and willing.

Wanted: Single person, preferably young adult male. Willing to work summer on wide, sandy ocean beach in quirky resort area. Possibility of high income with little effort. Potential party every night. Meet interesting and weird people and occasionally celebrities. Bikinis in abundance, male or female. Long hours so you can enjoy the job more.

Apply: White Cap Taxi, Fire Island. New York.

The above job description may sound fictitious, I admit to that. To the best of my knowledge this ad never appeared in any newspaper I read. I made this up. However, it does contain a kernel of truth and did prove to be marginally authentic. Through a set of questionable circumstances aided by relatives and friends, I landed a job as a driver with White Cap Taxi Service at one of the most extraordinary and bizarre summer resorts on the East Coast - Fire Island.

Lying less than fifty miles from the heart of Times Square and due east of New York City, the placid waters of the Great South Bay separate the island from the mainland. Its primary access is by boat. Geographically it's part of the greater metropolitan area. In all other ways, it's miles apart, off in its own ambiance, alone in a sea of outrageousness.

Notwithstanding the great diversities in communities and cultures, most Fire Islanders shared one thing in common. They came to relax, unwind, to let loose, to breathe deeply, and to take refuge from the urban grind, but not necessarily in that order. High on their priority list was partying. They needed a reliable, inexpensive taxi service for transportation. Moving people and their stuff was my principal preoccupation, but not my only consideration. During summers, sand, sun, booze and, of course, ladies had their own way of combining with each other to make for an excellent opportunity to be as hedonistic as one can get without fearing arrest.

What follows in the book is a recollection of my adventure; a "memoir" of sorts, of four summers on the island – 1960-64.

Fire Island is an unforgettable paradise for summer fun, a land of never-ending festivities, outlandish customs, bizarre attitudes, and heterogeneous populations. I loved it. While in residence I learned that partying was a verb, a way of life to pursue relentlessly, an active quest not to be disturbed by more mundane considerations. Taxi driving was merely an excuse to be there.

Fire Island, by comparison to the 60's is a different place today, a mellower place. The Gay Pride movement and political action initiatives of the LGBT communities have opened doors previously closed to homosexuals. Gays no longer are confined to intentional communities outside the mainstream. The "need" for an isolated gay enclave no longer is mandated and only exists by resolve and choice. More and more, gays and straights coexist side by side with little notice and even less alarm. To visit the island today, one would not recognize it as the wild and outrageous place described in the 60"s.

Perhaps the most visible and influential change during the last few decades is the demise of the beach taxi service. Along with their disappearance so also vanished a way of life on the island. That's been both beneficial and detrimental. The creation of the National Seashore Act in the mid 70's guaranteed the island's survival in its natural beauty as well as a heaven for an anxious and stressed population in need of respite from the urban grind. That's good. But it has also lost the freedom of adventure and ease of flow between its communities that so many thrived on during the decade of the 60's and early 70's that only White Cap Taxi service could provide. That may not be so good.

Although this episode of my life occurred decades ago, the memory of those four summers remains rich and lasting. The allure of the place remains deeply ingrained in my psyche as a spiritual and cerebral consciousness. In short, Fire Island, once experienced, cannot be easily forgotten. The story is true as best as I remember it. The episodes and opinions of the author reflect the attitudes of that period and are not meant to disparage any population.

1

Study in Contrasts

Through house-wrecking hurricanes (and parties).
Antediluvian restrictions (such as outdoor eating bans)
that labeled Ocean Beach 'the land of No', and zany
traditions (notably the mascara laden annual invasion of
the more sedate of its two gay communities by denizens
of the cheekier one, Fire Island has remained the ultimate
offshore getaway.

--A Resort of Dunes and Dreams, by Barbara Shea,
posted on Newsday.com, May 9, 2002

Tell just about anyone who lives east of the Mississippi
River and is over the age of thirty that you spent summers
on Fire Island, and they will presume you are gay. That's
the reputation the island has. I spent many summers on Fire
Island, but I am not gay (at least not yet). I am, however,
deeply indebted to the gay residents of Fire Island, thank
you very much. Without their support, patronage, and
eagerness to move about the Island, I might never have
attended graduate school and been able to pursue my chosen
profession. You see, I spent four summers as a taxi driver on
the island during my "formative" years (college is where
one's character is formed, so I've been told), and it was
primarily the gay community's patronage that provided

the funds for that education. But let me explain. A little background should be sufficient to clarify.

Fire Island lies roughly five miles off the south coast of Long Island, separated by the shallow waters of the Great South Bay. Water surrounds the entire island. A thirty minute boat ride across placid water and one arrives on the island. That's the most convenient way to access its communities unless one is willing to park at either end of the Island which are connected to the mainland by bridges, hike a few miles over soft sand, and trudge through poison ivy, beach plum bushes, and scrub oak while carrying all your needed possessions. Not recommended for the faint of heart and extremely time consuming.

People gravitate to the island for many reasons, not the least of which is its beautiful barren beaches, high sand dunes, warm ocean waters, and off- the- beaten-path locations. My mother and father never openly testified to their hankering for the beach, but it was the only place they ever spent summers. I never asked why.

From shortly after I was born, as soon as summer arrived, we relocated to the island. I didn't fully understand the attraction for my parents. Mom didn't like to walk, especially in sand. Sand was everywhere, so she spent most of her days in the house or sitting on the beach. Under those circumstances, she could have stayed at home and sat in a sandbox.

"I don't need to spend time walking here", she often told me. "What I want is to work on my tan. Vacations mean doing what you want to do when you want to do it". So Mom sat on the beach nearly every sunny day until her skin was roasted and looked eerily familiar to a catcher's mitt. When she wasn't sunbathing, she was drinking whiskey sours and eating raw clams, both of which she could do just as well back at home in New Jersey. Nevertheless, she couldn't wait to get to the beach each summer. An enigma in my book.

Pop's attitude was just the opposite. The beach was not a vacation, but rather a time to get work done, get "things squared away." If beaches have the propensity for encouraging relaxation, Pop had a funny way of showing it. Projects were his forte. The beach house demanded constant maintenance and he seemed willing, even anxious, to put in the effort.

"If I don't keep on top of these repairs, you kids won't have a summer house to come to," he often reminded us when we asked if he would take us swimming or hunting for soft shell crabs or fishing for snappers off the dock. "Be thankful I can do this work myself. A little gratitude, please", he added. I often wondered why we came to the beach all the time when it meant more work for my father. Eventually I realized that "working" was a significant attribute of his personality; work gave meaning to his existence. The beach house contributed to his welfare as much as it tried his patience.

There are no roads on Fire Island, no shopping malls, no high rise apartments, and no McDonald's. Today, Fire Island is part of the National Seashore administered by the U.S. Parks Department. Development is permitted only within the established communities, and these are located some distance from each other. In between, the island remains as it was decades ago, in its natural state. Residents and visitors alike clamber to its shores to revel in its isolation, its beauty, and most especially, its character. The island's ethos, tone, and complexion are unique.

Despite the natural beauty, I sense this is not its most ardent appeal. There is a practical function to the island, one to which environmentalists pay particular note. It is, after all, a long, skinny sand bar stuck five miles out in the Atlantic Ocean that acts as a barrier reef, sort of like a huge dam, to protect the south shore of Long Island from winter storms and hurricanes. Growing up on the island, we never gave these considerations much thought. Practicality and expediency are not the island's strongest selling point, certainly not reasons I could fathom. For our family it was simply where we spent summers, like it or not. For others, its lasting appeal was spawned by a reputation for harboring an eclectic assortment of people. Hardly a soul living anywhere between Manhattan and Montauk Point has not visited Fire

Island, or at the very least, heard rumors of the island's celebrated character. I suspect, however, that repeated portrayals about the island are not simple rumors, they are aberrations, slightly embellished renderings of the truth. For the greater population, I think these rumors accounted for its intrigue; that's what made it charming.

Throughout its history, Fire Island has attracted a wide diversity of populations. Coexisting at different times are clam diggers and fishermen, bohemian artists and urban professionals, old moneyed families and homeless squatter groups, young and single party seekers and old, cranky, in-bed-at-eight retired military personnel, straights and homosexuals. This diverse collection of humanity is squeezed into seventeen small communities

Fire Island lies relatively close, some say too close to New York City. From the center of Times Square, if one gets lucky and the Midtown Tunnel isn't clogged with cars, the island can be reached within three hours. Once on the island, you enter a world of little red wagons, high fashions, quaint cottages built from aged driftwood, days long parties, expensive antiques, chosen isolation, bathing attire optional, and a whole host of eccentric behaviors probably only barely tolerable to even the most liberal minded Middle Americans. It is a study in contrasts, a realm fully in both the 21st century and the 19th century simultaneously. People walk on ancient boardwalks in their up-to-the-minute modern fashions. Residents have few places they need to go and aren't in a hurry to get there as if they all emigrated from Amish country. There are no roads and automobiles are banned, but neither are there horses or steam engines. This is the preferable way of life on the Island, laid back.

Fire Island acts as a safety valve. It's an escape hatch, a refuge from the stress of city life, a deliverance from the work-a-day world, a place where even the most ostentatious person can be himself yet hardly noticed despite every effort to stand out. On Fire Island, people have learned to let it all hang out, literally and figuratively.

More than any other influence, it has been the evolution of the gay community that has garnered Fire Island's stature and prestige. At least two of the communities, Cherry Grove and Fire Island Pines, although different from each other, have achieved international recognition for their liberal attitudes. Both communities act as magnets for the gay, lesbian, and transsexual people of the greater New York metropolitan area. One writer on an internet blog shares the ulterior opinion of many residents and observers when he (or she) wrote *"As an owner of a house there, I can tell you that there are but two towns famous for their largely gay population, - the Pines and Cherry Grove. Those two are the places people think of when they hear the word 'Fire Island', and I therefore think of Fire Island as one, long, sandy cruising ground. However, I bet the Pines and Cherry Grove are a hell of a lot more fun and exciting (not to mention fabulous) than most of the other villages."*

Gays abound on Fire Island, but they aren't the only residents. The island is equally as notorious as a swinger enclave for the young and single (well, maybe not all single), those seeking the never-ending lure of new and brief relationships without consequences. Aptly called "groupers" for their chosen lifestyle of shacking up together to share rent, these folks loved their "sixish" cocktail parties (meaning they began somewhere close to the six o'clock hour) that only reluctantly broke up as the sun emerged the next morning.

Certain communities catered to the straight party clientele. Davis Park and Ocean Bay Park, for instance, epitomized the grouper life style where one could often find up to a dozen people sharing the rent of one cottage. My imagination went wild when I thought about the scheduling. What would happen if all the shared renters decided to show up at the same time? This arrangement made for some interesting experiences. As one visitor to Davis Park remarked, *"I come here to go crazy."*

A few communities have managed to retain the look and feel of a bygone century and reflect values characterized by middle class families, at least superficially. Point O' Woods, for example, is a fully self-contained, family-oriented village bordering on the sublime. As one resident stated, "Point O' Woods is a place frozen in time. " First conceived as an outgrowth of the Chautauqua Society; a cultural movement in the 19th century known for "wholesome" family entertainment, Point O' Woods became mired in its own righteousness. Residency is governed by such restrictions as a mandate that residents must have children and all homes conform to a single architectural style. A high-wire fence surrounds the entire village and access is restricted to inhabitants only. One wonders if the fences are to keep intruders out or residents in.

Still other villages are remainders of the past but much less sophisticated. Water Island, a community of less than fifty houses, has existed throughout the 20th century with no electricity, no running water, no garbage disposal, no shops, and one functioning telephone. Its population tends toward the blue collar types. The residents wanted to keep it that way.

At the far end of the habitation scale is Long Cove and Skunk Hallow, almost-forgotten communities at the eastern end of the Island. Originally founded by fishermen and clam diggers, many of the homes were constructed partially of driftwood found on the beach. Deeds to the land were non-existent or simply ignored and the residents became merely squatters. They had no plans to move.

How Fire Island got its name remains a mystery. Theories abound. Why people even care, also remains a mystery. For those inquisitors, the origin of the name gave rise to a great deal of speculation. According to Harry W. Havemeyer in his book, *Fire Island's Surf Hotel* at least two theories seem most plausible. The first claims that the name derived from the fires the native Indians lit who occasionally fished from the island. When they completed their days work, they lit a fire as a signal of their desire to return to the mainland. Kind of a "come and get me" fire signal. Havemeyer

A second theory according to Havermeyer's book was that the name derived from an early Dutch word. Apparently there were four small islands in the area around which Dutch seamen had to navigate so as not to go aground. The maneuverable inlet between them was known on Dutch maps as the "four island" inlet. The Dutch word for four—vier, meaning one more than three--sounded like "fier", which eventually became Anglicized as "fire". Referring specifically to this inlet, the land adjacent took on the nomenclature – Fire Island.

Havemeyer's theories, I am sure, are well researched. But they didn't stand alone, nor were they particularly interesting. Growing up on the island, I was influenced more by local legend handed down by my Uncle Paul who held no academic degrees but had a wild imagination. While gathered around marshmallow roasts on the beach, Uncle Paul informed that, yes, fires on the beach had much to do with the name Fire Island, but not Indian fires. Rather it was the lights from unscrupulous pirates and other outlaws who lit fires in the hope they would be mistaken as "lighthouses," luring unsuspecting cargo ships to run aground in shallow water. Once shipwrecked, these ships were fair game for looters. I personally spent many days over a dozen years hunting for buried treasure I was convinced was left behind by Blackbeard.

No roads; this might be among Fire Island's greatest charms. To be so close to the heart of the civilized world and be immune to the distractions of the car culture and its congestion, fumes, horns, engine noise, and parking problems is an enigma in the 21st century. Instead of automobiles, residents employed little red wagons for their minimal transportation needs. Each time a ferry landed, residents would load their groceries and other paraphernalia into their wagons for transport to their beach houses. Confusion often arose over the ownership of the little red wagons since they looked so alike, but more often than not, such encounters served as excuses for people introducing unfamiliar folks to each other. "Borrowing" someone else's wagon often was the first step toward being introduced to a new friend. The "pull" to leave a neighborhood, to go somewhere else for entertainment or company, was minimized by the fact that there was no way to get anywhere outside of walking or owning your own motor boat.

White Cap Taxi changed all that. The attitude of isolation, once so prevalent, soon gave way to a yearning to explore.

The attraction of the "gay life," epitomized by those living in two specific communities – Cherry Grove and Fire Island Pines – became the motivation for the sudden urge to travel. Like a magnet, these communities attracted the curious and the inquisitive. The very folks, who previously accepted the "leave us alone" attitude, were among the most ardent in utilizing the new transportation system. Despite that residents fought tooth and nail against any efforts to build a road, beach taxis met little resistance. Like the chicken and egg dilemma, however, it was difficult to decipher which attitude preempted; if the taxis encouraged beach travel or the desire to travel encouraged the taxis.

White Cap Taxi service began accidentally and somewhat naively. Two local men, Roger Miskowsky and Everett Wright, brothers-in-law, enjoyed coming to the island for fishing and duck hunting. Everett built himself a squatter's shack at Skunk Hollow. To get to their favorite fishing and hunting spots, they converted old Model A Fords, the kind with large flywheels, into cut down beach buggies by adding oversized balloon tires for better traction in soft sand. They drove them to the island during winter months over the Smith Point Bridge far down at the east end. After a splendid day of fishing or duck hunting, what better way to complete the experience than to celebrate with a little bar hopping? Friends tagged along. Soon these same friends were asking for help transporting furniture and lumber from the ferry docks to their homes on the island. And after a hard day of construction work, these same friends requested rides to different restaurants that were opening on the island. More requests – getting to church services on Sunday mornings, transporting groceries, delivering messages – came pouring in. Eventually it dawned on the brothers-in-law that their taxi services could be a cash cow.

By the late 1950's White Cap Taxi service was officially born. Used four-wheeled-drive Willys painted red with a white top replaced the Model A Fords and revamped military vehicles. The owners installed short-wave radios so that drivers could talk to each other as well as with a base station located in the up and coming hub of island transportation, the community of Fire Island Pines. The radios allowed drivers to roam the beach and still be in touch with a dispatcher for acknowledging pickups called into the office. By the time I joined in the effort in 1961, nearly a dozen of these jeeps were put into commission, and the business was a fulltime operation from late May until after Labor Day.

Working as a White Cap Taxi driver was not my first introduction to life on Fire Island. I was practically born there, and if not for World War II, I might very well have been born there. I was born during July, 1941, the only year in recorded family history when my parents did not spend the summer on Fire Island.

I abandoned summers on the island when I first started college for the sake of working at jobs in various locations. That lasted only two years. I returned to take the job with White Cap Taxi. It was shortly after my stint as a taxi driver that my parents sold our house on Fire Island for the meager sum of twenty thousand dollars. Today, that same property, thanks to the formation of the National Seashore Act, is probably beyond the financial reach even of Bill Gates (probably not true, but very expensive nonetheless).

The National Seashore Act served to protect the island much as it was and will do so in perpetuity. White Cap Taxi, however, didn't fare as well. It's long gone, but not forgotten. I feel fortunate to be among the very few who drove a taxi on Fire Island. The experience proved to not only to be an ideal summer job, but also an introduction to a culture I only imagined existed.

2

Not Just Any Beach

*This scent's barrier island namesake, ninety minutes
from Manhattan by train and ferry, is the hideaway
where New Yorkers come in droves to let their hair
down and uncover their skin. Fire Island may be made
of sand dunes, but it's got distinctive New York-esque
neighborhoods (Kismet...Saltaire...Atlantique), a heavy-
duty night life, shopping (natch), and a history, in the
1920's,as a Bohemian retreat. In other words, it's home
not too far away from, home. So it's a legitimate part of
our scent repertory.*

--advertisement for Fire Island
by Bond #9, a fragrance

I couldn't sleep the night before our annual big adventure.
The anticipation was way too much and kept me awake past
midnight. The next morning was the day we were to leave
for Fire Island. The excitement was overwhelming. I had
been through the same routine many times before, but each
time felt like the first time. I couldn't wait. Even now, many
years removed, the recollections of our trips to Fire Island
loom large and recurring in my memory.

Our journeys to the beach were not one day affairs. We
went for the whole summer. Dad didn't always stay the
whole time because of his work schedule, but Mom and

my brothers, cousins, and friends survived from shortly after school let out until school opened again in the Fall. My parents may have considered other options for summer vacations, but they never shared those thoughts with us kids and we always ended up at the beach, our beach, at Fire Island.

Being at the beach wasn't like a vacation for me. I never envisioned it as a holiday. I read about other families where everyone piled into the family station wagon and took off for destinations I only dreamed about but never visited such as Yellowstone Park or Disneyland. We didn't take trips to exotic places; we only went to Fire Island. The house at the beach was my second home. It was the only place I ever spent summers, and I never tired of it.

Preparing to leave for a whole summer was a complex ordeal. It was a marathon undertaking. The initial challenge was the car trip from our home in Jersey to Long Island where the ferry then carried us across the Great South Bay to Fire Island. We planned to depart shortly after Memorial Day. Organization was crucial. School had to be officially dismissed for the summer. Mom had to cancel and reschedule her circle of club meetings. Pop had to arrange his portion of time off with his brother, with whom he shared a retail flower business. Since we would be gone for at least three months and not return home until after Labor Day, arrangements for mowing the lawn, canceling the newspaper, watering the plants, feeding the animals, and returning library books had to be completed. My brother's and my priorities were considered trivial matters; Little League games were not important, swimming lesson at the Y could be rearranged, and friends we played with would still be there when we returned. "Don't give me any grief cause we're leaving anyway," Mom insisted whenever we mentioned summer events we had planned with our friends, such as swimming lessons, sleepovers, muskrat trapping, or fishing trips at the nearby lake. We only mentioned these concerns to gain attention, to let our parents know that we had lives of our own. Actually, and I suspect my brothers would agree, we would gladly postpone these for the opportunity to go to the beach.

Although I knew I would be bored and anxious to return home by the beginning of September, the expectancy of getting ready was a source of great anticipation and utter confusion. Packing had to be completed and the car loaded the night before. I would pack at least two suitcases, usually with stuff I knew I couldn't spend a whole summer without – underwater face mask, three kites, a cowboy hat, cowboy gun, holster and caps, my collection of adventure soldiers, and a ton of comic books – only to have my mother unpack half of it, claiming there was not enough room in the car for all this unnecessary junk. I didn't think it was unnecessary and I certainly didn't think it was junk.

Most important to my father was that we leave before the sun came up the next morning. Getting an early start was his perception of "getting squared away," by which he meant anticipating every possible delay (bathroom breaks, traffic congestion, flat tire, walking the dog), and any imaginable catastrophe that might beset us that would cause us to miss Pop's chosen ferry departure time. There might be four ferry departures for that day, but the eleven o'clock departure was the only one he would consider. Getting to the ferry on time meant a very early departure. Essentially an anxious person, my father projected, almost expected, disaster and delay. I think if no calamity occurred, Pop felt cheated.

I remember one year on the night before we were to leave, a loud crashing noise woke us up at about four o'clock in the morning. I recall thinking about the worst-case scenario: that my older brother finally got so frustrated with my parents that he shot them. When the sun came out and we all assembled outside, we discovered lightening had struck a corner of our house. There was minor damage and some shingles dropped in the driveway. It wasn't the damage to the house that troubled Pop; it was the disruption in his scheduled departure time. According to him, we now had to "waste" an hour or two cleaning up the debris. I could see the despair on his face and hear the anguish in his voice.

I wasn't as much bothered by this calamity, however, as I would have been if my brother had actually fired that shot. Leaving later than sunrise left too little time for Pop's mandate of activities scheduled for the remainder of the first day. Most years, by six in the morning, Pop, my mother, my two brothers, Frisky the dog, and I were loaded in the black two-door 1948 Ford sedan with a stick shift on the floor, and we were eager to go.

Frisky hated the car. I suspect that being cooped up in the back seat for the two and half hours it took to reach the ferry caused her great anguish. Frisky made sure my father suffered along with her. No sooner had we left the driveway, than Frisky would begin to pant ferociously and slobber and drool and jump about in the back seat. This annoyed Pop to no end.

"Keep that damn dog sitting down and in the back," he yelled. "I don't want her sticking her nose up front and panting the whole way. It distracts my driving. Sit down, you stupid god damn mutt."

"She's not bothering anyone," my mother said. "She can't help it. She's excited. She's just a dog and does what dogs do naturally." She attempted to rationalize the situation. Pop did not respond as a rational man with three kids and a dog in the car while driving through the crowded streets and highways of New York City.

"The damn dog is slobbering down my neck," Pop would bellow. He swung his right arm backward forcefully; he hit the dog across the chest, and Frisky tumbled toward the back seat and ended up on the floor. Immediately she would be up again, start panting and bouncing around, and the whole routine would repeat itself.

"Damn dog, why do we have to take the dog," Pop would reiterate repeatedly for the entire trip. I felt Pop actually loved the dog except for car trips.

If it wasn't the dog annoying Pop, it was we kids.

"How much longer?" we repeated every ten minutes. "I got to pee. Edwin's sitting too close to me. He's breathing on me. Frisky needs a drink of water. Paul took my comic book without asking." There must have been a million questions and complaints and petty annoyances, or at the very least, as many as we could fit into a two-and-a-half hour car trip. With scheduled stops along the way, which Pop tried to avoid, but relinquished when we convinced him that pee would not make the car smell good, and the occasional unscheduled catastrophe, the trip normally stretched closer to three hours. If there was excessive traffic especially on the George Washington Bridge or the Queens Midtown Tunnel, depending on Pop's route that day, the whole three hours or longer went beyond stressful and approached calamitous. Pop had zero tolerance for traffic jams and wasn't shy about relating his frustrations. Rarely did he confront the other drivers directly or exhibit obscene hand gestures; instead he either mumbled under his breath just loud enough for us kids to hear, "God damn it to hell; what's the matter with that asshole" or he would swear at us kids as substitute antagonists. I would hear words from my father's mouth that I don't think were in any dictionary. Mom would gasp and reprimand him when hearing such language.

"George, the kids are in the car and you need to watch your mouth. You just work yourself into a dither for no reason," she would tell him

My parents lectured my brothers and me often about how fortunate we were to have a house at the beach when other kids, like those we passed in the Bronx, had to spend their summers on the front stoop of an apartment or in the streets in front of their tenement building.

"You kids should thank your lucky stars," Mom would remind us, "that we give you a nice place to spend your summers. These kids have to play in the street. They get no attention from their parents like you do and don't get out of the city all summer. You get the ocean to swim in and they just get a fire hydrant."

When we passed these kids and I saw how much fun they seemed to have playing stickball in the street or being doused by open fire hydrants and noticed their multitude of friends, I sometimes wished I was one of them. I especially got jealous when we passed Yankee Stadium and wondered how often these same kids got tickets to games or just snuck in. I pined for the adventurous life of the urban dweller.

My grandmother lived near the ferry landing on Long Island. It was routine to stop there for a brief visit and it meant free food. It also meant she cajoled me to rest my head on her bosom, which was ample, as her gesture of showing how much she loved me. This little exercise of affection became more uncomfortable the older I got. By my teenaged years, I managed to stay outside with my brothers and waved to grandma through the window.

Nearby, Uncle Harvey had an old-fashioned general store that sold everything from soup to hardware. He specialized in providing necessities for people living over at Fire Island where there were no stores. Groceries where phoned in from the island, packed up in his store, delivered to the ferry, and then retrieved in little red wagons once they arrived at the beach. Pop's schedule always included a visit to Shand's General Store for supplies prior to boarding the ferry. We couldn't survive even a few days without ice, kerosene, Coleman lamp wicks, and parts to fix the pitcher pump. In addition to shopping, there were family stories that needed reiterating. Uncle Harvey knew all the gossip about relatives who we saw infrequently because we lived so far away.

I grew up on Fire Island, and would have been born there, if it weren't for the threat of World War II and the fact that I was born in July 1941. I never knew whether my parents shied away from the beach that summer because of the threat of war, or because my mother was pregnant with me and didn't want to venture far from home. Did my parents fear the Germans or did they fear giving birth in the sand?

Our summer habitation of Fire Island went far back in our family's history. My mother's father had a profitable lumber mill on the shore of the Great South Bay across from Fire Island. From stories told to me, my grandfather didn't have a fondness for Fire Island - too much sand and not enough whiskey - but he did have a yearning to be a sea captain. He loved his yachts, of which he had a few.

He was rich by the standards of his day and indulged his children with boat trips across the bay to the island. The kids liked to spend days cavorting on the beach and evenings entertaining friends with parties on the yacht. The grainy old photos my mother pulled out periodically, when nostalgia overwhelmed her, showed both she and my father posing on the bow of some boat, usually with drink in hand, docked somewhere at Fire Island. Summers must have been cooler during the 1920's. People in the photographs were dressed in full length bathing suits that looked like they were made of wool and showed little skin other than arms and legs protruding. I could only imagine the suffering they endured on hot summer days for the sake of modesty and fashion.

Mom and Pop met at Fire Island and later got married nearby under problematic circumstances. They eloped. Only afterward did Mom's father catch wind of it. His reaction was underwhelming. It took some time for fences and feelings to mend.

The year 1938 was not kind to residents of Fire Island. It was the year of the most devastating hurricane to hit the East Coast in a century. At its highest elevation, Fire Island is slightly below twenty feet. We estimated wave surges during the height of the hurricane at over thirty feet. It doesn't take a genius to figure out that flimsy summer cottages were no match for the fury of that storm. My mother showed me pictures of Cherry Grove after that hurricane.

"See that old refrigerator lying in the sand next to the bricks? That was all that was left of your grandmother's house after the storm," she told me. Seeing these pictures of a destructive hurricane sent shivers up my spine. It affected my perspective on any approaching summer storm. While staying at the beach in our house, I had nightmares every time the weathermen predicted a storm might be approaching. One year, Hurricane Carol rolled in after midnight. We weren't able to evacuate the Island and had to ride out the storm in a neighbor's house situated higher up on a hill. I watched intently, scared to death, as waves swirled around the base of our house down below. Following that storm, the nightmares increased until, as a teenager, I outgrew the fears.

After the hurricane of '38 the greater part of Cherry Grove remained as smooth as a baby's bottom. Hardly a house endured, dunes were devastated, and the beach front was reduced to half its size. But Fire Island was in my family's blood. Storms of any size did not sway them to abandon the place. Hurricanes were minor annoyances or diversions. For the next few summers (except the year I was born), my parents rented a home in the community of Ocean Bay Park. I have no memory of time spent there, but have seen old photos of myself during those years. My brother appears old enough to be in a real bathing suit, but I am always in diapers. I imagine my bottom as rubbed raw after sitting in the sand attired only in my wet diaper. I have a hat on in each picture. You can't see my face. My mother claimed that my face blistered badly in the sun and the hat kept me from looking like I had leprosy. Only my bowed legs which I still possess identify me.

My grandfather didn't hold a grudge for long. When Mom and Pop found a house on the beach they wanted to buy, Grandpa lent them the money. The home was in a different community –Water Island-- that once harbored a grand old hotel that had burned to the ground decades before. The charisma of the community had long ago vanished with the hotel. What remained were a few summer cottages and a strong middle-class family atmosphere. The isolation and primitiveness of the community contributed to residents' self-sufficient attitudes. People liked having no electricity, no running water, no ferry service, no garbage collection, and minimally imposed regulations. It was to here we moved and remained every summer for the next twenty-five years.

Our house stood only a couple hundred yards back from the ocean, hidden behind low sand dunes. The surf was clearly visible and even more audible from the second-story windows. One of the most pleasant memories was bedtime. With the windows open, I could clearly hear the sound of the waves cascading against the sand. The rhythm of the waves lulled me to sleep as no sleeping pill or copious amounts of beer could ever do.

The wood-framed house stood off the sand about seven feet on locust posts. The architectural concept was that the posts were rot resistant and held the house above high water in case of a hurricane. Never imagining the possibility of another hurricane, Pop enclosed the area between the posts with chicken wire and stucco to create a kind of encased cellar. It was here that we stored the rowboats, fishing tackle, tools, pitcher pumps, window screens, ropes of all sizes and lengths, pipes, and assortments of junk my father deemed "useful" someday. The cellar became the perfect imaginary room. I spent hours here with friends rearranging the piles of assorted crates, anchors, ropes, tools, and fishing gear to form forts and barriers from which we fought off imaginary enemies. Hurricane Carol eliminated the cellar, filled it with sand, and our house became a two, rather than a three-story structure after that time.

Beach houses presented unique problems. Water, for instance was always a challenge. Not that there was no water or too much water, but finding water suitable for drinking took some innovation and persistence. We drew water for drinking from a well by pumping the handle of a pitcher pump screwed tight to the top of a long iron pipe which had to be forcibly driven with a sledge hammer down into the sand below the house. Our pitcher pump was located in the kitchen above the sink, the usual place for such an apparatus. The location, however, made it difficult to work on when maintenance was needed. My father and his friend Carl Krauth were most adept at this chore. Karl was a big, burly man and Pop always waited until Karl was available since the hammer used to drive the pipe was particularly heavy. I watched in amazement as my father would hold a flat 2 by 4 plank on top of the iron pipe while Karl swung the huge hammer and beat on the plank over and over forcing the pipe into the sand. Taking aim with the hammer seemed not to happen. Karl swung it blindly and rhythmically but never missed the top of the plank. Slowly but surely, with each swing, the pipe was forced further into the sand. I watched with great trepidation, fearing that the hammer would strike my father in the head and die right in front of me.

The routine of driving the pipe happened often throughout the summer months. The problem occurred with the rising and falling of the tides. Fresh water is lighter than salt water. If there was a particularly higher than normal tide, the salt water forced the fresh water to rise above the bottom of the pipe and the pitcher pump filled with salty water. The point or bottom of the pipe no longer stood in fresh water and needed to be raised higher. Just the opposite occurred when the tide was particularly low. The depth of the fresh water table constantly moved up and down and the point of the pipe protruding into the water and had to be constantly moved higher or driven lower. A real pain and a constant source of irritation for my father and I'm sure for most other's with similar water setups.

Water coming into the house also had to find a way out of the house. Another real pain was the cesspool. High tides and general neglect during the winter months left the septic tank--a hole in the ground enclosed by bricks--completely full and dysfunctional. Once the top was lifted each spring, the foulest smell emerged I had ever experienced. It knocked your socks off if you were wearing any. It had to be emptied out--a labor-intensive and really malodorous task--before more wastewater could enter. My father attached a bucket to a rope and lowered it into the cesspool. He then retrieved the bucket, walked a few yards away and dumped it onto the ground. The dry sand absorbed it almost immediately. After a number of dumping's, however, the area began to smell and became squishy and Pop had to walk further and further away to deposit the sludge. Pop repeated this routine as many times as necessary to empty the cesspool. Sometimes, this took my father half a day. Once again, I heard language from my father that Mom censored as unfit for children's ears.

Because Pop abhorred the task of emptying the cesspool, he was fastidious about how water flushed down the toilet. He cautioned all, better yet threatened all, not to flush the toilet after each pee.

"It's unnecessary," he announced almost daily. "Pee doesn't stink that much and all that water just fills up the cesspool and I got to clean it out. No flushing unless absolutely necessary,"

I got very adroit at flushing the toilet. After a few pees, I learned that it would flush with only a quart of water if poured in from a height of three feet or more. Pop used me as a model protagonist for his water conservation environmental assessment program.

"See," my father said. "See how Peter flushes. That's the way you all need to flush."

"What about craps?" my brother would ask.

"Flush only if it's necessary," was Pop's reply. "That's all I'm saying." We were left to ourselves to make that determination, knowing that the crapper god would shit on us if we were wrong.

We wore no shoes at the beach, or at the very least, they were optional. But there were consequences for going barefoot. The boardwalks were exactly that--walks made of boards. Wood deteriorates over time and splinters from rotting wood occurred often. Having a splinter in your foot was less than disastrous, but having it removed by Mom, well that required considerable bravery. The anticipation of the needle was the worst of all.

"It has to come out," Mom would tell me. "Otherwise it could get infected, you might get gangrene, and then your foot has to be amputated. You don't want that, do you? So sit still. Did I ever tell you about the boy who didn't tell his mother about a splinter?"

"Yes you did," I responded. "Every time I get a splinter, you tell me about that boy and what happened to him. Can I meet this boy sometime so I know you're telling the truth?"

"Just be quiet and sit down." She would point to the table on the back porch known as "the gurney," Removing splinters was either major or minor surgery, depending on one's perspective, the patient's or Mom's. Needles or safety pins substituted for scalpels. Sterilization consisted of holding the point of the pin over a lit match. Anesthesia was for sissies only. Cries of "Help, I'm being murdered," were heralded from the agonizing patient but ignored by my mother.

Pop owned our house, but he chose to share it with my uncle Paul and his family for reasons beyond my comprehension. The two brothers were in business together and each spent his allotted vacation time at the beach house at different two-week intervals The two families minus the fathers, however, were often together at the house causing minor conflicts: who gets to sleep where, who has to do the cooking, whose rowboat belongs to whom, and "Those are my swim goggles and you can't use them."

Neither Uncle Paul nor my father was good about taking vacations. They each envisioned being at the beach house as a time to get things done, or "squared away," as Pop was fond of repeating. Translated, that meant keeping things ship-shaped. Nothing was allowed to remain broken or past its scheduled maintenance. Lying in the sun or lazing around the beach was wasted time. Napping after lunch on the front porch or occasionally surf fishing were the only recreational events I remember Pop allowing himself to enjoy. I hardly remember any time at Water Island enjoying the amenities of beach life with my father outside of helping him paint the house, assisting him to repair a boardwalk, or watching him empty the cesspool.

Life evolved differently for me as I entered the age of puberty. In elementary school, I was content to play war games in the cellar, row my boat looking for crabs in the bay, or pick beach plums, read comics, or fish for snappers. When puberty arrived with intensity and a new set of hormones set in, life changed drastically. By the time I was fourteen or thereabouts, two priorities guided my every thought--girls and driving. Learning to act cool was the motivating force and being cool meant knowing how to drive, and knowing how to drive was what girls wanted from cool guys. Both were actions after which I lusted eagerly.

Although girls were plentiful, opportunities to drive on the island remained rare. Hence, the prospects for showing my "coolness" were not available. Having no roads and very few vehicles was a drawback for me, but a boon for the rest of the residents. After all, that was the attraction of the island, no automobiles. Consequently, the only vehicles were the occasional contractor's four-wheel-drive trucks and plumber's jeeps. Whenever the smell of gasoline permeated the air anticipating the arrival of an approaching jitney, I would halt any endeavor I might be involved in, with a girl or without a girl, and run to the head of the dunes to peer at the passing vehicle with the excitement of a toddler on Christmas morning.

Despite my enthusiasm, I didn't have a driver's license. I was too young. Actually that mattered little. Without roads, there were few regulations and even fewer authorities to enforce them. Anyone of any age with a functioning beach buggy could drive. My parents were the main opposition.

"No, we can't bring our car over here and no you can't drive it even if we did," my father reminded me each time I pestered him about converting our old Chevy to a beach buggy for the summer months.

Next door lived a boy a few years older than me. Johnny Marin showed up one summer with a stripped-down Model A Ford equipped with the mandatory balloon tires for soft sand driving. I don't remember asking how it got there, whether by barge or driven over the Smith Point Bridge. Either way, there it was, parked next to his house. It was a beauty. The rear seat was removed and replaced with a flat wooden bench. The covered cab had been cut away to make it a convertible. No license plates appeared on the front or the back, but who cared about minor inconveniences. It was in the optimum condition for travel on the beach.

How I envied Johnny. Not yet sixteen and already he had his own beach buggy with no restrictions on when or where he could drive.

"How fast can she go?" I asked him.

"Dunno," he said.

"Can you drive her anytime you want?"

"Yup. So long as I got gas.

"But your father owns an oil company.

"Don't mean I don't have to pay for it.

"Ever get it stuck?"

"Nope."

I kept up the questions to Johnny about his beach buggy as foreplay to gain enough nerve to ask him for a ride, or in my imagination, to ask if I might drive it. No matter how much I pestered him, no invitation was forthcoming. My persistence eventually paid off. One day while Johnny was changing the oil and adjusting some bolts on his buggy and I was hovering nearby, he turned towards me and said,

"Want to go for a ride as soon as I get her running?"

"Yeah. Sure." I repeated it. "Yeah. Sure."

Residents maintained a cut through in the dunes in those early days at Water Island. It provided access to the Burma Road, allowing builders and plumbers to park next to the houses they worked on. After one of the winter storms that came later, it was closed to traffic, but jeeps still drove over the dunes where the cut used to be. Johnny finished his maintenance and cranked up the Model A. It started immediately and hummed like a food processor. The smell of gas fumes further excited me.

"Get up on the back and hang on," Johnny told me. I jumped up on the flat wood bed of the buggy.

"There's nothing to hang on to," I told him.

"That's your problem. Find something to hold to," he replied.

Johnny let out the clutch and the buggy jumped forward with a lurch. I grabbed the side of the wood frame with both hands and laid flat on my stomach. He drove along the Burma Road, over soft sand hills, and across the low brambles that protruded into the path. I hung on with all my strength as the buggy bounced and swayed with great exaggeration. We reached the old cut in the dunes and Johnny roared over the top and headed down toward the hard-packed sand by the water's edge. The tide was low. He turned back toward Water Island and picked up speed. I smiled as I anticipated that some of my friends might be on the beach. I wanted to wave to them as we passed by and gloat in the jealousy they surely would feel. It was a big deal to be riding with Johnny.

I turned from the back bench to face forward to get a glimpse of where we were heading and who might be in front of us. As I shifted my weight, the buggy suddenly hit a sluiceway, a hole in the hard sand washed out by receding water, leaving about a one-foot drop off. The rear of the buggy must have jumped three feet into thin air. It flipped me upwards and by the time I came back down, the buggy had passed from under me. I lay face down in the sand. Water was washing over me and I felt sand full down in my pants. I wasn't hurt that I could tell, only humiliated.

I stood up and watched Johnny and his buggy still moving with great fleetness down the beach. He either didn't know I fell off or didn't care. He approached the kids on the beach, waved to them, and they waved back. My opportunity to gloat was gone. I had to walk the half mile back to Water Island.

"Where have you been?" my friends asked as I approached along the beach.

"Just went for a walk down by the dunes looking for beach plums."

"You missed Johnny," one of them told me. "He must have been doing fifty in his buggy when he went by."

"Yeah, I guess he was," I said. My embarrassment and badly bruised ego kept me from further humiliation.

The jeep ride only encouraged my desire to someday be able to drive myself along the beach front, a dream that eventually came true a few years later.

3

The Perfect Summer Job

Summer's lease hath all too short a date.

—William Shakespeare, *Shakesphere's Sonnets*

I knew I had to have a summer job. Not that it consumed my every thought, but it was expected of me, so I had to give it due consideration. I was in college and responsible for helping defray my school expenses. My parents did not have lots of money and wanted me to learn responsibility; they lived at the edge of the income scale, and my school expenses were not their top priority. Other than when I was in elementary school, I always had a summer job. By the time school let out in the late spring, a summer job felt like a welcome alternative to studying. But not all summer jobs were equal or desirable.

The ideal summer job is a matter of personal perspective. I suspect my perspective was different from most others. I was an aspiring college student, a young stud seeking the adventurous life. The criteria for summer work had to exceed the mundane. Yes, the paycheck needed to be adequate, the challenge minimal, and the work almost effortless. Promotion was of little consequence since the task was so short-lived – summer only. Wherein lays the priority? It's with the circumstances. For me, the ideal summer job needed to be associated with the summer environment – parties, girls, beer, sun, and surf. Not necessarily in that order but not much else is required.

I have had some interesting, but uninspiring summer jobs since junior high. I sold vegetables at a road-side fruit stand. I hung rugs to dry in a commercial laundry. I picked up trash from the beach, mowed lawns, washed dishes, and set out beach chairs. When hired as a life-guard at an exclusive country club, I got really excited. The job seemed promising with the hope of bikini glad girls in abundance but proved less than inspiring. The girls were there, but I couldn't inspire them. Each of these jobs seemed ideal when I started. In many cases, however, I was history after the first week. I didn't enjoy the job. I wasn't growing rich. I didn't meet girls. There were no parties. If it's a summer job, what's the point if you can't have fun in the sun.

One day while on spring break from college I received a phone call.

"Peter," the woman on the line said, "it's your Aunt Ethel." Aunt Ethel was my mother's older sister. She lived on the south shore of Long Island across the Great South Bay from Fire Island. She also had a summer cottage on Fire Island. I only saw her during summers while we resided at the beach. When we were there I spent much of my time with Harvey, my cousin who was my age.

After some pleasantries and small talk about how the family was and when was she going to see me again and information about Harvey, she said, "The reason I'm calling you is I have a friend at Davis Park who runs a beach taxi service during the summer. He told me he was looking for people to drive. It's Everett Wright. Do you remember Everett?"

I didn't remember but said I did to encourage her to continue.

"Well anyway, he told me he needed drivers and I said my nephew might be interested."

"What about Harvey? Is he interested too?"

"No. Harvey is staying up in Syracuse this summer. He's working some job at his college and that's where his girlfriend is. He's preoccupied, if you know what I mean."

A few years had passed since I last spent a full summer at Fire Island. I lost touch with what might be happening there and did not remember much about the taxis. I asked Aunt Ethel to tell me more.

"Everett and his brother-in-law, Roger, at least I think he's his brother-in-law, run the White Cap Taxis. You know: those red and white jeeps that run up and down the beach front. I think they have most of them at Fire Island Pines. I know they take people down to Cherry Grove on week-ends. Everett told me he needed some drivers for this summer. If you're interested, let me know. Better yet, I'll give you Everett's phone number. Wait just a minute. I have it here somewhere."

There was a pause for a few moments while I suspected Aunt Ethel was looking for the number she thought she had somewhere.

"You still there?" she said as she returned to the phone. "I have it right here. Do you have a pencil and paper handy?"

"Yup, I'm ready." I wrote the number down and repeated it back to Aunt Ethel just to make sure I had it right. One digit incorrect and I'd never reach him. She asked to speak with my mother so I handed the phone to Mom.

I tried to recall what I remembered about the taxi service. Not much. Water Island, the community where we spent summers on Fire Island, was a small community and somewhat isolated. People liked it that way. We once had a direct ferry service, an old clam boat that came by twice each week and delivered a few people and groceries from Shands Market on the mainland. Most residents had their own boats. The ferry service discontinued for lack of customers. The ferry schedule tended toward the erratic. Most residents claimed that was because the captain imbibed a bit too often. Our family was one of a few that relied on the ferry for transportation and grocery delivery. I remembered my parents telling me that since the ferry quit, they were now getting groceries delivered by jitney from Davis Park. That started during the few years I was absent from the Island. I had no idea of the extent of the taxi operation for the rest of the island, at least not until after Aunt Ethel's call.

I learned that the taxi service was a recent phenomenon. Two brothers-in-law who enjoyed coming to the island to hunt and fish began it unintentionally in the early 1950's. Everett Wright and Roger Miskowsky drove a couple of used Willys Jeeps to the Island on weekends. Their intent was to transport themselves and a few friends to the better fishing spots and duck hunting areas. After a long day of recreation, they willingly drove their friends to some of the bars along the island for an evening of frivolity. Soon, the frivolity became a priority of their friends, and the brothers-in-law recognized a cash cow when they saw one. In addition to bar hopping, they were often asked to transport furniture, groceries, and appliances that came over by ferry but were too cumbersome to be pulled to the residents house by the traditional little red wagon.

The phone call from Aunt Ethel intrigued me. I called Everett Wright that very evening.

"Mr. Wright," I said. "This is Peter Olsen. I don't know if you remember me from Water Island. My Aunt Ethel, Ethel Shand, said I should call you about working for the White Cap Taxi this summer." Before I could explain my intentions any further, Everett interrupted.

Ethel Shand, Yeah, I know Ethel Shand. How is she? Is she over at Davis Park now?" He continued to pepper me with questions about Aunt Ethel. Then there was a slight pause.

"What did you say your name was?" he asked me.

"Peter, Peter Olsen," I responded.

"And why are you calling me?"

"My Aunt Ethel said you might need a driver for White Cap Taxi this summer."

"Yeah, we need drivers," Everett said. "Have you ever driven here on the beach before?"

"No," I told him. But I knew I needed to establish some connection or credibility. "But I am familiar with Fire Island.

I grew up there." Then for some unexplained reason I added, "I have driven a school bus."

"A school bus," Everett repeated. "That's a lot different than driving a taxi on the beach. But give me your phone number and I'll let you know."

I gave him my phone number. I repeated it three times before he got it right.

"I got it," he reassured me.

"You can reach me any time. I'm always here," I told him. That was a lie but I wanted to impress him with my responsibility. I heard Everett hang up the phone.

I immediately knew the school bus inference was a complete blunder. What was I thinking? I thought that maybe a letter would be convincing, you know, tell him about how mature I was, the summer jobs I previously held, give him some references, let him know how wonderful my mother thinks I am, stuff like that. I thought I might end the letter by telling him that if I didn't get this job I might just kill myself. I thought pity a great motivator. I never finished the letter.

Over the next few days, despite not knowing what the job really entailed, I constructed my own spin based on my vivid imagination. With my mind in creative overdrive, I imagined having my own taxi and working for White Cap. Each morning about 10:00, I would arrive at work in a tee shirt and bathing suit. After lathering up with sun-tan lotion, I would spend many hours lounging on the hood of the cab working on my tan. I would stop periodically along the beach, as the mood dictated, for an occasional swim in the warm waters of the Atlantic Ocean. A pretty coed of college age and intelligence – forget about the intelligence – would accompany me in the passenger seat, unless it was needed by a paying customer. There would be a different party each night. My mother or Aunt Ethel would insist on cooking me free meals. Two days off each week would be satisfactory. No traffic. No congestion. No sweat, or maybe a little from the warm sun on my body. I ran this scenario through my mind over and over again until I convinced myself this would be the picture-perfect summer job.

Back to reality. By the middle of May Everett had not called back. My anxiety level rose considerably. I began to think, following our first conversation, that he sounded too noncommittal for me to assume the job was mine. Why hadn't he called? A couple of options crossed my mind. Perhaps I should call Aunt Ethel again and ask her to intervene. Everett clearly had much respect for her. If this sounded like I was "using" Aunt Ethel, well, so be it. I wanted that job. Or I could call Everett directly. I could use the ploy that I was just checking with him now because I had other offers for summer jobs, very lucrative jobs, but out of consideration, wanted to give him first priority. A bold faced lie, but I was becoming desperate. Or maybe he lost my phone number and I was calling just so he wouldn't be disappointed when he was unable to reach me. All of the above scenarios began to sound lame, but the suspense and apprehension of not knowing was killing me. I had to call.

Everett answered on the first ring. "Mr. Wright, this is Peter Olsen. I talked with you a while back about driving for White Cap this summer. I was just wondering."

He interrupted me. "Peter who?"

"Peter Olsen." I repeated my name slowly and emphatically almost spelling it. "Ethel Shand's nephew. I wanted to…"

Again he interrupted. "Ethel Shand. I know Ethel. How's she doing?"

"I guess she is fine. She sends her regards." I lied again. I hadn't spoken with Aunt Ethel in over a month. "I'm calling about the job driving for White Cap. I'm really interested."

There was an awkward pause. I couldn't tell if he cut me off or he didn't understand me or perhaps he was searching for specific words like, "Don't need anybody, and certainly not you even if I did need someone."

Then Everett spoke before I could. "I thought I told you last time, if you want to drive just come over to Davis Park and I'll get you started. Do you have a chauffeur's license?"

"How do I get that?" I asked.

"Where do you live? He asked

"In Jersey,' I told him.

"Well you need to get the license somewhere in New York State. You have to have that license to drive a taxi, even here on the beach now. It's a pain in the ass, but the cops have been checking our drivers more each year. So get the license and come out to Davis Park as soon as you got it. I gotta go now." He hung up.

A whole new dilemma emerged. I had to get a chauffeur's license and I had no idea of what this would require.

4

The Chauffeurs License

Officer: *"How's your driving record?"*
Bickle: *"It's clean, real clean, like my conscience."*
Officer: *"So, whaddya want to hack for, Bickle?"*
Bickle: *"I can't sleep nights."*
Officer: *"There's porno theatres for that."*
Bickle: *"Yeah, I know. I tried that."*
Officer: *"So now what do you do?"*
Bickle: *"I ride around most nights – subway, busses –*
but you know, if I'm gonna do that, I might as
well get paid for it."
--*Taxi Driver* (1976 Martin Scorsese movie)

There are no roads on Fire Island, only sand, lots of sand. For those seeking the recreation of a surfside vacation, this sounds like paradise. But to the beach taxi driver, it's a major obstacle. If you drive, you drive in the sand. Speed is not an option. Soft sand has the propensity of slowing a vehicle down, and the inclination to sometimes veer too close to the surf and ending up in the waves, makes driving on the beach a major challenge.

Once there was a road, a least in name. Locals called it the Burma Road. There is no known connection between Fire Island's Burma Road and the country of Burma (now known as Myanmar). To call it a road may be a misstatement. Actually it was just a bumpy pathway that allowed jeeps to move over the marshland, across shifting sand dunes, and through the scrub oak that grew in abundance where there were no houses. The Burma Road lay inside the dunes, which is to say it was not exposed to the beach front or the ocean waves.

During the Second World War, the government fabricated the Burma Road. The Coast Guard positioned stations about every five miles just inside the dunes along most of Fire Island. The road enabled Coast Guard personnel to travel between the stations undetected from off shore. The government thought, in their wisdom, that the east coast of the U.S. needed some defense against the threat of German U-Boats that might be plying the Atlantic Ocean just off the South shore of Long Island. The government feared that if the U-Boats got too close, spies might swim ashore. This was all highly unlikely and only speculation. I suspect if that ever happened during the summer months, the spies might have enjoyed the beach as much as the residents, and after joining in a clam bake, downing a couple of cold beers, and sharing a bit of sunbathing, preferably in the nude, they probably wouldn't want to swim back to their U Boats, and instead apply for sanctuary. No serious consideration was given to this circumstance. Protection was paramount. More likely those stationed at these lonely outposts used the road to transport beer and food undetected from their own authorities since no warfare ever occurred on the island and life could be rather boring, especially during winter months.

After the war, the road remained. It became the primary right of entry for plumbers delivering propane gas tanks to summer cottages, the access point for carpenters to get materials close to houses under construction, and a means for jeeps to deliver boxes of food to the isolated communities ordered from Shand's Grocery Store. Construction crews built boardwalk bridges over the road so as not to impede progress.

The Burma Road also served as a metaphorical link between communities sometimes separated by miles of undeveloped land, sand dunes, and low lying scrub bushes. Because vehicles were rare on Fire Island and the lack thereof often gave people a feeling of isolation, the road symbolized a connection. Whenever a jeep or jitney (slang for a small bus or unlicensed taxi) traveling the Burma Road approached a community, it turned into a happening. People gathered on the overhead boardwalks waiting for the vehicle to pass underneath. Such a gathering was a social event. There was only so much isolation an urban dweller could take before a "fix" of vehicle traffic and gas fumes became a welcome reprieve and an excuse to mingle with other people.

These "bridges" over the Burma Road were also great jumping off places for kids who pretended to be paratroopers, allowing them to land in the soft sand below. Unfortunately it wasn't always soft.

When Clarence the plumber would bring propane tanks to our house, he had to pass under the boardwalk bridge. It was a scheduled service call, and we usually knew when he was coming. In anticipation, some of the more daring amongst us would wait on top of the bridge for Clarence's flatbed four-wheel-drive pickup to pass underneath. We imagined Clarence as an enemy soldier preparing to carry our parents away from the island and place them permanently in a concentration camp. As official Water Island Rangers, it was our task to avert this catastrophe. Because of the soft sand, Clarence drove slowly. Just as he passed under the boardwalk, the more daring of us would leap from the board walk in an attempt to land on the flat back of his truck. Sometimes we were successful, sometimes not. Either way, it hurt. Clarence was a good old boy who enjoyed the thrill of the adventure as much as we did.

One needed no license to drive the Burma Road or anywhere else on Fire Island prior to the 60's. Soon afterward the state mandated licenses for commercial taxis. In those early days, the island was immune to prohibitions against vehicle regulations. Anyone with a revamped Ford model A with balloon tires or used army jeep with altered insignia could drive the beach. It wasn't that the law allowed them; the law simply ignored them. The Island remained license free until White Cap Taxis service began to operate. I didn't think I needed a license to drive a beach taxi. But attitudes changed, and I soon learned I did. Police presence on the Island had increased recently. Enforcement of driving regulations intensified. The Burma Road closed. Driving over dunes was prohibited as an insurance against erosion. County police intensely monitored beach front traffic. To drive for the White Cap Taxi Company, I had to get a special license, a New York State Chauffeur license.

Getting the license proved more complicated than I imagined. Only the Motor Vehicle office of New York could issue it. I lived in New Jersey. Travel into the city was always inconvenient. Busses were reliably late, trains only ran during rush hours, and parking a car in New York City costs more than renting a two-story town-house on Fifth Avenue. I decided to drive and take my chances double parking.

The law specified that I meet certain qualifications for achieving the status of Chauffeur. I had to be an upstanding citizen, not committed murder in the past six months, have a clean driving record, and prove that I sent a Mother's Day card during the last year (I made up this last one). I also had to pass a written test

Tests hated me. Tests were my adversary. I never met a test that liked me. Perhaps a bit of an exaggeration notwithstanding, however, I still held tests in great contempt, but I always acted respectfully when in their presence, and spoke favorably of their significance. Regardless of these considerations, the conclusion was always the same; they still managed to fail me one way or the other. Fear of failure was a constant nemesis for me and caused many sleepless nights. Taking the Chauffer's license test was not an option; however, it was a mandate. I had to prepare myself. Increased anxiety often resulted in nausea. Throwing up in the office of the New York Department of Motor Vehicles would only result in embarrassment; certainly not create empathy.

As I drove though the Lincoln Tunnel from New Jersey toward Manhattan, it dawned on me that I could have asked them — NY Department of Motor Vehicles— to mail me a study manual rather than my having to drive into the city.

But that didn't happen, and I soon was looking for a place to double-park in lower Manhattan. I found the Motor Vehicle office, picked up a chauffeur driving manual, and prepared to leave as quickly as possible to avoid a ticket. I had to pass only the written test and not the driving test. The study manual posed many regulations pertaining to driving on two-and four-lane roads, knowing the difference between a yield sign and a stop sign, and when to turn right on a red light and when not to. It seemed redundant to me since there were no roads on Fire Island, no stop signs, no red lights, and it would be a rare occasion to even see another vehicle. But bureaucracy is a necessity, I suppose. I acquiesced, picked up my drivers manual, and returned to Jersey ready to study.

I was in college and studying was a priority that lay far below beer drinking, chick chasing, and sleeping. But I gave it my best. Instead of Chaucer, I read about Chauffeuring. I replaced my need to read about Modern Africa with an attentive eye toward taxi protocol. I memorized the requirements for how many people can "legally" fit into one taxi. I learned to only pass in safe zones, never sit idling on railroad tracks, and to check my rear view mirror before pulling out into moving traffic. It was all totally irrelevant and unnecessary information for beachfront driving. After diligent study of the manual cover to cover, I asked my friend to test me. He asked questions. I gave answers. I got half the answers correct.

The following Monday morning, I took the train into Manhattan. This trip I avoided driving because of the increased prohibition against double parking and the anticipated need to remain longer. I imagined the examiner in the Motor Vehicle Department informing me that I passed the test, but because of the ticket I just got for double parking, he would have to rip up my test.

The examiner was pleasant but curt, a middle aged white women with heavy smears of lipstick that made her look as if she were perpetually smiling. She had a lit cigarette in the ashtray on the side of her desk. She spoke with a typical New York accent. "The sodar and cawfee machine are ouside" she told me. She wasted few words but spoke with authority. "Whadda ya wawnt" she asked me when I first presented myself at the front of her desk. I told her I was here for the exam, and then asked "What do I need to do?"

"Here's your examination booklet," she told me. "Youse can sit over there and tell me when youse are done. And don't forget to mawrk each circle fully wid this pencil." She handed me a number two yellow pencil. I asked for a second pencil just in case I broke a point. She looked at me as if that was a great imposition, an intrusion. With pursed lips outlined in glowing red, she clucked her tongue, reached into a side drawer, and thrust a second pencil toward me point first.

"Thanks" I said, glad she didn't stab me, and sat down at one of the desks in the dark corner she assigned to me.

The actual test questions were easier than those my friend had asked. A few questions were technical. "How much liability insurance is required for a commercial taxi?" I had a choice of four possible answers. (1) None. (2) One thousand dollars. (3) One million dollars. (4) All of the above. A second technical question proved even trickier. "How often is a taxi required to be inspected?" Again there were four possible answers. (1) Once a year. (2) Once each quarter year. (3) Every lunar eclipse. (4) None of the above. I had no idea. I remember guessing at answers but I don't remember the actual test contents.

I handed my test back to the examiner. I don't know what she examined, but she wore a little pin on the front of her blouse that said "Official MV Examiner." I assumed that she wielded some power over who passed exams and who didn't. I respected that.

"I got a few things to do before I score your test," She told me. "Youse can have a seat over there." She pointed to the dark corner again.

I looked around the office as if searching for someone. I wanted her to know I knew no one else was present in the room.

"Don't be a wise ass," she said. "I'll call you when I'm ready" They graded tests by hand back in 1961.

I sat in the examination room about twenty minutes reading old copies of *Quail Hunters Magazine* and the *National Geographic*. The seats were hard wood. My butt began to hurt so I got up and walked around the office and read the notices on the walls. "No personal checks accepted" and "Bathrooms are for Employees only" were the most noticeable.

"Mr. Olsen, Peter Olsen," she called out.

"I'm here." I responded. I was the only person in the room so the announcement seemed redundant. My adrenaline was running rampant and I could feel my heart beating in the back of my throat. I immediately stepped directly in front of her desk, standing only a few inches away from her face. I think I frightened her. She instinctively pushed her chair back as if fearful I was about to attack. I took a step back.

"I'm sorry," I said. "I'm Peter Olsen," Besides her, I was still the only other person in the room and don't know why I chose to identify myself again.

"I know, I know," she said. She looked down at my test lying on her desk. She flipped to the second page and then back to the first page. Her face appeared inscrutable, almost poker-faced. I couldn't tell from observing her facial expression if the news was good or bad. She had a yellow pencil poised in her hand as if she were about to write something on the test. Instead she tapped the eraser end continuously on her desk. Tap, tap, tap. I watched her brow furrow and eyebrows rise and fall almost rhythmically with the taping of the pencil.

"Please let it be passing," I mumbled softly.

"What did youse say?' she asked and looked up at me.

"Nothing," I replied. I then added, "I had a cold and felt a cough coming on. Haven't felt too well the last few days." I was so anxious I could feel nausea about to erupt.

Again she pushed her chair back a bit from her desk. "Youse got six wrong answers," she said. "Do youse want to know which ones?"

In the most dejected voice I could muster I said, "I suppose so."

"But you still passed," she said. "You're allowed eight wrong."

"Good," I said, but wanted to blurt out "Yes, Yes," while thrusting my fists in the air.

I refrained myself from bear-hugging her and kissing her on the forehead. The feeling of humiliating myself stifled my actions.

"Thank you. Thank you very much. You have been most helpful and I love you" It just came blurting out spontaneously.

That brought the first smile I saw on her face. I think my outburst shocked her, but she still sounded appreciative.

"Youse still haven't said if you want me to go over the questions you got wrong," she said.

"No, I am sure you must have other things more important to do." I tried to be as charming as I knew how in my euphoria. "I'll look them over later." I lied.

"We will mail youse a temporary license in a few days and you'll receive your permanent one in two weeks," she told me.

"Oh take whatever time you need," I said. I felt such relief and joy that I would have succumbed to any suggestion or request she might have made, even willing my first born male son to her. Now I wanted to get out of there quickly before she recounted my missed answers.

5

Apprehensions – First Day on the Job

Cab drivers are living proof that practice does not make perfect.

--Howard Ogden

The envelope looked very official. It had the seal of the State of New York imprinted on the upper left hand corner. I immediately ripped it open. With hands shaking, I feared it might be some kind of rejection notice and not the license I was expecting. Maybe they found out I had placed gum on the back of the movie theater seat when I was ten, or that I had hit my older brother in the head with a coke bottle when we were playing war games, or even worse, that I left my wallet on the seat of a pickup up truck my friends and I took for a joy ride late one night at a construction site. But how would they know? The government knows everything.

No, it wasn't a rejection. Inside a single piece of paper embossed with a small circular seal of the Motor Vehicle Department authorized me as a fully licensed chauffeur. On the opposite side were my picture and a list of a few conditions: "Good only for three consecutive years and not valid without corrective glasses." I construed this as my official license to drive a taxi. I could now actually and legally charge people to drive them places.

"That's bullshit," my friend Brian said when I showed him my newly acquired chauffeur license. "The way you drive, you couldn't pay me to ride with you."

"This is on the beach out at Fire Island, stupid," I responded. "It's not in New York City."

"They got taxi cabs on the beach?" he asked. "Who you gonna drive around, clam diggers and fisherman? "

Since I knew Brian didn't have a summer job yet, I asked if he wanted to go with me to Fire Island and see if a taxi job might be available for him.

"Naw," was his answer. "Sounds like a lot of sand in your underpants."

Brian helped me get my old '54 Chevy I inherited from my parents into shape for the trip out to Long Island. The Chevy had deteriorated significantly since I got it as a gift after my father acquired a new car. Unlike myself, Brian had a knack for working on cars, and he was extremely reliable.

I was prepared to leave the first week of June, but by doing so, I knew our beach house would still be shuttered and closed down the way my parents and brother Paul had left it the previous fall. We put on hold the family tradition of taking a weekend right after Memorial Day and dedicating it to opening the house for the summer season because my mother had feigned sickness. I suspected otherwise as she never enjoyed the work and hoped that my brothers and I would do the honors without her. Shutters had to be taken down, water siphoned to prime the pumps, furniture taken outside and hosed down to remove the accumulation of mice turds, moth balls removed from bed linens, and beds made up. The odorous task of cleaning out the septic tank was always a favorite. My brothers were not available to help, so the task was mine to open the house if it was going to happen at all.

Living at the beach house would not be under optimal conditions. Having a clean house was not a priority for me, so the living conditions mattered little. What mattered was that I would have to cook for myself, a task I dreaded. My abilities at cooking were extremely limited, intentionally so because I so abhorred it.

My first stop before taking the ferry across to the beach was at my Aunt Ethel's house in Patchogue. She lived on the mainland during winter months but moved to the island early in the summer.

"Would it be all right with you if I leave my car here? I might use it occasionally when I need to get off the beach." I asked her.

"That's fine. Just don't leave it where the neighbor kids might get to it."

"Not to worry, it's a piece of junk already. They can't do much more to it,"

"They might take the whole car," she told me. "That sort of thing has been happening a lot around here lately"

After my Aunt Ethel graciously offered the back yard of her house as a place to park my car for the summer, I asked diplomatically if I could stay at her house on the beach.

"I was also wondering if I could stay with you for a while until I can get the Water Island House opened up and Mom and Pop arrived," I asked her. It appeared as a lop-sided exchange, but sounded reasonable to me. She got my car in her back yard and, in exchange, I got to eat her food. She reminded me, however, that staying with her at her beach house was not an option since she was expecting other family members soon who would be staying for much of the summer.

I knew very little about being a taxi driver and even less about who ran the service. I decided to pump Aunt Ethel for information.

"Well he doesn't have many teeth left," was my aunt's first response when I asked her to tell me what she knew about Everett Wright. "I think Roger is his brother-in-law,"

"Who's Roger?" I asked.

"Roger is the other guy who owns White Cap Taxi. I don't know him well, only met him a few times." She paused a moment than added. "He's a big guy and I hear he's got quite a temper."

The words, "He's got a temper" caught my attention. I've noticed that people use that phrase sparingly but intentionally when they want to convey some personal bias, but not directly. The "I hear" part keeps this opinion from being subjective, personal, and judgmental. I have difficulty deciphering exactly what they mean. Is the person easily angered, but basically harmless, or do they mean the person is slow to anger, but when aroused, keep your distance? The combination of "he's a big fellow" and "he's got a temper" raised my anxiety level five degrees above comfortable. I went to bed that night wondering if I was in over my head.

Aunt Ethel and I took an early morning ferry across the bay to Davis Park. Despite being in her 60's, Aunt Ethel had recently secured a job as the first postmistress for this seasonal community. Like myself, she was about to start a new job. Aunt Ethel had left her little red wagon by the dock. We loaded some groceries, her suitcase, my backpack, and an old oil lamp on to my aunt's red wagon. She treasured that lamp because it came to her from my grandmother. I pulled the wagon up the dock and onto the board-walk heading toward Aunt Ethel's House. The board-walks had loose planks which caused the wagon to bump as it rolled.

"Be very careful with the lamp," she kept reminding me. "Your grandmother had that in her front room for years. It's an antique." I had remembered as a child how residents on Fire Island loved to import antiques for their houses. I think it gave them a feeling of quaintness in their summer cottages.

After helping Aunt Ethel carry her baggage to her cottage and successfully not damaging the lamp, I left my own backpack with her and made my way back to the ferry landing. I asked various people-a man washing the deck of his boat, another trying to catch crabs with a fish head on a rope, another carrying a dead horseshoe crab, and one more who was loading up his own little red wagon with bags of charcoal-if they knew where I could find Everett Wright. All of them said they knew Everett, but hadn't seen him that morning. I gave up and returned to Aunt Ethel's. It was lunch time.

"Everybody knows Everett, but no one knows where to find him," I told her. I felt somewhat frustrated.

"Yeah, he's hard to find. You know, he's often hanging around the Casino. I think he works for them part time, sort of like a maintenance man."

The Davis Park Casino was an older, wooden framed building perched precariously atop the dunes, and, after many winter storms, looked almost as if ready to collapse onto the beach front as the sand beneath got constantly blown away. Tall locust post reinforced the back portion, a recent addition. *Just one more summer* has always been the mantra of the owners of the aging casino.

I headed to the casino. More anxious thoughts began to reemerge. Since I told Everett of the day of my arrival, I half expected him to meet me at the ferry landing, to welcome me to the job, and to present me with my own set of keys to a taxi. I needed that assurance but wasn't getting it. It felt like a bad omen when I had trouble finding him. Perhaps he found someone else to take the job and didn't feel obliged to notify me. Or maybe he just didn't need any drivers. Or perhaps I had convinced myself of an ideal summer job that simply didn't exist. I was preparing myself for impending disappointment. I always do. That way when the worst happens, it feels less devastating.

I went inside the Casino bar. A man was picking up cups, glasses, empty beer bottles, and emptying ashtrays. The room reeked of stale alcohol and stank of putrid smoke.

"Excuse me," I said. He didn't acknowledge me or respond. I raised my voice and again said, "Excuse me."

That got his attention. He looked up and then at me. His frazzled hair, unshaven face, and swollen eyes convinced me he must have been there all night.

"Sorry to bother you," I said.

"No bother, brother," he responded. I was surprised at his pleasant retort despite his appearance. "What can I do you for?" he asked.

"I'm looking for Everett Wright."

"Well ever since he stopped drinking, you won't find him in here. I suspect he's probably around back, under the building, fixing something or another. He always finds stuff to fix whether it needs it or not." He walked out back with me and pointed down under the building. "He's down there probably storing propane tanks. That's his jeep parked there."

Since the back end of the Casino rose nearly fifteen feet off the sand and was open to the air, gas propane tanks could be located there. I descended a set of rickety stairs to ground level. I was moving in on Everett and getting more nervous.

A short, stocky man wearing a dark brown shirt and brown work pants with deep side pockets (the style and color of a Nazi uniform) and a brown baseball cap was hefting a five-foot tall propane tank, nearly as large as himself, across the sand under the building. He rocked it back and forth as he "walked" the tank into its position next to a few others already positioned there. I watched from a distance until I saw he had it securely and safely situated. Perspiration beads had formed on his forehead and were beginning to flow down his face. Just as he pulled a soiled handkerchief from his pocket and began wiping his brow, he noticed me standing nearby.

"Are you Mr. Wright," I asked?

"That's right, I'm Wright. You got me." I could see a lot of missing teeth as he spoke.

"I'm Peter Olsen. I'm supposed to be working for you driving for White Cap this summer." I started to ramble on about my writing him and reminding him that he said I could have the job and that I just got here and I was staying with my Aunt Ethel, until he interrupted.

"You got your license?" he asked. He wiped his hands on his pants. I figured he was about to reach out for a handshake. Instead, he pulled a candy from his pocket, unwrapped it, and popped it into his mouth.

"Do you want to see it?" I asked.

With the candy rolling around in his mouth, it was difficult to decipher what he said, but I think I heard, "Don't need to do that. Besides it's your hide if you get caught."

"No, I really do have my license. I left it at my Aunt Ethel's house. I can get it for you." I felt obliged to assure him

I was legal even though it seemed not to matter to him that I prove it. This surprised me because he had been emphatic about having a chauffeur license if I wanted to drive for White Cap.

"The cops check for the license ever since we started this business," he explained after he swallowed the rest of his candy. "People who don't like taxis on the beach are always bitching to the cops. They think we drive on the dunes and break them down, so don't drive over the dunes unless it's through a cut. I had one cop check my license last week even though he knew I had it. They like to harass us. Gives them something to do. Don't usually see cops on the beach unless there's been a drowning or murder."

It was more information than I could absorb all at once, but I did interpret it as an affirmation that I had the job.

"I got to finish up here," he continued. "Come down by the docks in about an hour and I'll get you into your taxi. You can start driving now, right?"

"Sure can," I answered. "Right away." I reminded him that I was staying with my Aunt Ethel.

"Ethel Shand," he asked? "I know Ethel. How's she doing? You know she's the new postmaster or whatever you call a lady postmaster. Real nice lady." This felt like a conversation I had before. When I left, Everett continued wrestling with the propane tanks and I felt a lot more comfortable about having a summer job.

After Aunt Ethel and I shared a drink, I then walked down to the ferry dock. Everett's head was buried in the engine compartment of a red and white Willys jeep parked alongside the docks. I knew it was him because I recognized the brown shirt and brown stained pants. Painted on the side of the jeep in white letters was "White Cap Taxi." The jeep looked like a big box on wheels with dents and rust covering most of the fenders and side panels

Everett must have sensed my presence. He pulled his head from under the hood, wiped his hands on his pants, and said, "This jeep is gonna be yours. It needed a battery. It's not new. Otherwise she should be in good condition and it should last you a while. I worked her over pretty well this winter and she's been running fine. But you gotta take care of her."

We both looked inside the engine compartment. I didn't know what I was looking at, but I wanted Everett to think I was interested. It all looked confusing to me. Various round containers and greasy things stuck out from the engine block and wires crisscrossed along the top like a huge spider web and hoses spaced helter skelter connected various parts of the engine.

Everett asked, "Where are you living this summer?"

"Right now at my Aunt Ethel's, but as soon as I get our house opened up at Water Island, I'll be there,"

"You know you can't get inside the dunes at Water Island anymore,"

I told him I knew that. "Does that make a difference?"

"Means you got to park on the beach next to the surf and the engine will get pretty damp there and probably hard to start in the morning. I don't want to have to come down there every morning and get you started. Can't you stay at Ethel's? You can bring the jeep inside here at Davis Park."

"I'm not sure she will want me there all summer. I haven't talked with her about that. I think she has guests coming for much of the summer." Right away, I thought I was not being cooperative and maybe putting this relationship in jeopardy. "But I will ask her again," I added. I already knew this wasn't a possibility.

"Yeah, well we'll try it at Water Island and see how it works," Everett said. The tone of his voice indicated misgiving.

Everett got in the Willys jeep, and after pulling levers, pumping the gas pedal a few times, and looking very serious; he attempted to start it. It turned over unsuccessfully a couple of times and then roared to a start. He gunned the engine two more times, black smoke burst from the tail pipe, and then he shut it down. He had a look of satisfaction on his face.

"She's good to go," he said as he slipped out of the driver's seat. He handed me the keys. You'll be working with Roger down at the Pines, I'll radio him and tell him you're coming, so go ahead and get down there."

"Right now," I asked?

"Yeah, now.

"You want me to drive to the Pines now?" I asked again.

"Yeah, "he said again as if he'd forgotten he already said that once.

My speculation about having the job was over, but my anxiety still mounted. I was expecting, at the very least, a brief orientation period before starting the job. I wasn't sure how that might be accomplished, perhaps a couple of days of supervised training while riding with one of the other experienced drivers, some information about taxi etiquette on the beach, a schedule of dates and times I was expected to work, paperwork to sign, and the usual tax forms to fill out. There was none of that. Just get in and start driving. I'm on the job now. Despite my apprehension I thought it best not to ask unnecessary questions. It would only serve to show my witlessness, and Everett might conclude that I was too much a novice to be entrusted with one of his taxis.

Everett interrupted my train of thought. "There's a cut in the dunes just east of the casino," he told me as he pointed in that direction. "Watch out for boards with nails in them," he added. "And stay out of the surf."

Now it was my turn to get into the jeep. I paid close attention to what I was doing as Everett remained hovering nearby. I felt overwhelmed by all the instructions and even more by his expectation that I was now ready to be on my own in one of his taxis. I had the overwhelming feeling that now was not a good time to screw up. It wasn't a particularly warm day, too early in the summer, but sweat beads formed on my forehead.

My nervousness didn't lessen as I turned the key and the engine started immediately with a roar. I noticed black smoke emitting from the rear. I also noticed how closely Everett was watching and talking at the same time but the noise from the engine kept me from hearing all his words. I did catch once again his mandate, "Watch out for boards with nails."

It was time to move. I shifted into first gear, popped out the clutch, and instantly the taxi jerked forward, came to an abrupt halt, and the motor stalled. Everett had a pained look on his face. I restarted the engine. This time I gave it considerable more gas until the motor roared and once again let the clutch out, but more slowly. The back wheels spun mightily, but I went nowhere. The soft sand absorbed the rear tires as if on a cushion of soap suds. I was stuck.

I looked over at Everett who was shaking his head in the manner of someone who has just realized that he has confronted an idiot.

"You don't have her in four-wheel drive," he yelled at me. I then stalled the engine once again. He reached in the cab and pointed to a lever sticking up from the floor boards. "This here is the four-wheel drive lever. Pull it up and leave it up." He sounded a bit frustrated.

I pulled the lever up and started the engine again, and slowly let out the clutch while gently increasing the engine speed. My heart felt caught in the back of my throat and sweat continued to flow down my brow. This time was a do-or-die experience. I knew it might be my last chance to show I could actually drive the damn jeep. The taxi lurched forward with great halting and jerking movements until I got the speed under control. I was moving and Everett was in my rear view mirror, slowly but surely becoming a smaller and smaller figure. I felt some relief.

I followed the well-worn jeep tracks in the direction Everett had pointed toward the cut in the dunes east of the Casino. I shifted into second gear. I was determined to keep the taxi running and moving, at least until I was out of Everett's sight. I stayed in second. Shifting more gears was too risky. I headed up over the cut, but could hear the engine laboring as I encountered deeper and softer sand on the upward incline. Still in second gear, I gunned the engine full throttle. I felt the taxi accelerate and literally race over the top of the dunes and start down the other side. I was fast approaching the beach front.

The ocean was directly in front of me, less than a hundred yards distance. At this pace, it would only be a matter of seconds before I was awash in the breaking waves. I turned sharply to the right, feeling the taxi tilt precariously, but managed to stay upright while missing the wave with only a few inches under my tires. I headed the jeep closer towards the dunes away from the surf and brought the taxi to a halt without shutting down the engine. I then let out an elongated sigh and curled my tee shirt over my forehead to wipe the sweat away. Everett's words, "Stay out of the ocean," remained only as an afterthought

6

"I Told You to Stay Out of the Ocean"

Water is the driving force in nature.
—Leonardo da Vinci

Life begins at the end of your comfort zone.
—Neale Donald Walsch

It was summer. I was on one of the most beautiful beaches on the East Coast. I had my own jeep, a dream coveted since I fell off the back of Johnny Marin's beach buggy ten years previously. I was a full-fledged and duly licensed taxi driver. Everett was behind me, now long forgotten, despite that I only left him a few minutes ago, and I was on my own. The ultimate summer job I had so long fantasized about had become a reality. Sand, sun, surf, my dreams had come true. Life was good, but sometimes you have to be careful what you wish for.

I left Davis Park and rode along the beach-front. The tide was low. I could see that the sand closer to the water's edge was hard packed and solid. My new found ability to keep the taxi from stalling in the soft sand up close to the dunes bolstered my confidence. I left the soft sand tracks and steered down toward the water's edge. As I approached the hard packed surface, I could feel the engine relax, its strained laboring noise morphed into a monotonous hum. Without any effort to accelerate, it increased speed on its own as if it felt a sudden freedom from constraint. The engine whined and second gear was no longer sufficient, so I shifted into high. The ride was smooth and fast. All the windows were open. The ocean was immediately to my left only a few yards distant. A slight breeze entered the opened windows, freshening me from the warm afternoon sun. Sweat left me. The salt air lingered in the cab eradicating the smell of gasoline. Sea birds scratching for small crabs along the water's edge scattered as I approached.

My mind raced back to my earlier expectations. I recalled last April wondering what beach driving would be like. So far I wasn't disappointed. The thought of a full summer cruising the beach boosted my feelings of euphoria after such a disastrous beginning. My imagination roared into overdrive as I considered the summer's possibilities: the sun gently tanning my skin, the ocean readily available when it got to hot, bikini clad girls, beer-drinking beach parties, and clams, crabs, and fish for breakfast, lunch, and dinner. This must be Nirvana, I thought.

For this I was being paid. Well not yet, but that was my expectation. I hadn't seriously considered the salary circumstances. Everett hadn't mentioned anything about salary and I felt too intimidated in his presence to inquire. I didn't want to appear too assertive. For the meantime, it felt sufficient to know I had a job despite not knowing about my salary. The time and circumstance would come later, when I would feel more confident, to consider the logistics of salaries and working hours.

I was heading west toward the community of Water Island, where I had grown up and where my parents still owned our summer house. My mind wandered as I thought about the many times my brother and I would make a day of hiking from Water Island to Davis Park, a distance slightly less than two miles. It was never just a straight journey; there were detours and stops along the way. We explored the old Coast Guard station that was abandoned shortly after the end of World War II, climbing the rickety stairs that remained attached to the old tower, peering into some of the abandoned Coast Guard resident quarters, and imagining what it might have been like to look for German U-Boats. We wandered the dunes with the hope of spotting a deer or some rabbits. Often we used the journey as an excuse for picking beach plums, which we sold to my uncle at Shand's Grocery Store. These distractions transformed an hour's walk into a full day adventure. Through soft sand, each mile of trudging felt like ten miles. We never tired of the adventure.

I didn't realize how close Water Island really was while driving along the hard packed sand next to the waves. I was approaching our house after just a few minutes driving time. Again my mind wandered as I thought about our beach house at Water Island. Was there any damage from the winter storms? I'd have to rid the house of mice before sleeping there. I wanted to stop and have a look around before proceeding to Fire Island Pines further down the beach. If I could at least get the house open, even though barely habitable, I could manage to stay there. That would mean opening windows, getting water in the pump, and lighting the kerosene refrigerator at the very minimum. I hesitated to do these tasks now; best wait a few days. I decided to stop and at least have a look to see if any damage occurred from winter storms. I glanced toward the top of the dunes hoping to spot the roof of our house.

Without warning I was suddenly jolted in my seat. My head flung forward as I felt an enormous shudder at the front of the taxi. Instantly water doused the windshield so completely that I couldn't see through it. Water splashed in through the open windows, soaking my tee shirt and pants. My glasses fogged up, and I could not see where I was heading.

Instinctively I swerved to the right, away from the surf. The engine had stopped, but I had enough momentum to carry me forty feet up on the soft, dry sand. The taxi came to an abrupt halt as it settled down. "Oh shit," I said aloud, my usual spontaneous outburst when detecting a pending disaster.

I tried to restart the engine. There was a grinding noise as the engine turned over and over but wouldn't start. No noises other than the starter engine slowly giving up the ghost as the battery wore down. Steam wafted out of the engine compartment, a result of cool ocean water contacting the heat of the engine block. A slight breeze blew the steam away. I wiped the salt spray from my glasses as I contemplated what to do next.

I recalled the advice I received from Everett no more than a half hour ago. "Watch out for boards with nails in them and stay away from the water." I had my first encounter with an ocean wave, and the wave got the better of me, not an auspicious beginning for my first day on the job.

I was stuck, literally and figuratively. The jeep was stuck in place; it appeared hopeless it would start again soon. Even worse, I felt I was stuck in a dilemma. How could I ever explain to Everett why I never made it down to Fire Island Pines? Thirty minutes on the job and I had broken a cardinal rule: I got too close to the water and found myself marooned on the beach.

That helpless feeling was overwhelming. I got out of the cab and wandered aimlessly around in the sand muttering "Oh shit, what the fuck am I going to do now?" I felt disoriented and bewildered, feeling unable to function and consumed by a mental haze. No solutions to my predicament seemed forthcoming. I felt engulfed in my own desperation.

I was within walking distance of Water Island. The first boardwalk seemed only a few hundred yards ahead, and I could see the roof of our house as it protruded above the dunes. Like a small child when confronted by something dreadful, I headed toward home as if the familiarity of our beach house might provide some solace.

At the top of the staircase leading up from the beach, my eyes focused on the Browns' house, one of our neighbors. I noticed their shutters were off and their windows open, a sure sign that they had arrived for the summer. I walked past our own cottage and headed straight up the hill to the Browns. Surely I could find some assistance from old family friends. I approached the house, walked around back, and found Buddy, the oldest son, cutting weeds. He acted surprised to see me.

"Hey, what are you doing here?" he said. "You're early. You guys don't usually come until later in June."

Buddy, despite being about my age, didn't have a summer job. Instead, he helped his parents around the house and occasionally cut brush in people's back yards or painted houses at Water Island

His real name was Eugene, Eugene Willard Brown, but we all referred to him as Buddy. He was a large, gangling guy, with an infectious laugh. None of my brothers or friends or I, sought Buddy out as a special friend. Most times we tended to avoid him. His gangling and goofy mannerisms, combined with his appearing somewhat slow, gave us the impression that not all his porch lights were functioning, that he might have had a severe blow to the head when he was younger. Either way, despite that we never invited Buddy to hang out with us; intuitively he knew where we were and just showed up when least expected.

"Whatca doing?" Buddy would say. Whatever we were doing, Buddy inevitably asked "Can I do it with you?"

Being brought up to tolerate all kinds of people, we relented and included him in our endeavors if for no other reason than he was always good for a laugh. Because of his infectious belly laugh, he encouraged others to laugh, not at what was said or what had happened, but rather just because he was laughing. No matter what the circumstances -- falling out of a rowboat, soda dripping out our noses, pulling up a crab hanging onto the fish we just caught, tripping over the edge of a chair, or being knocked down by an unsuspecting wave – Buddy thought it was hilarious. Much of the time my two brothers and cousin Harvey intentionally mimicked the antics of the three stooges just so we could laugh at Buddy's laugh. Buddy was a great audience. None of us admitted it, but we also included Buddy in our company because he provided a connection to his younger sister who we all thought was stunning.

Before I could tell Buddy about my predicament, he started with the questions.

"Are you here for the summer? Where are your brothers? Want to go for a row later. Did you bring any beer? "

"I got a job this summer driving taxi for White Cap," I told him. I hesitated to reveal this because his father, Captain Brown, a well-respected island resident, made it known publicly that he emphatically opposed any driving on the beach. I never had positive proof, but suspected that he was responsible for some of the boards with nails in them that showed up in the wheel tracks of the soft sand where beach buggies often traveled.

"Right now, I got a problem," I continued. "My jeep is down on the beach. I hit a wave and the water knocked the engine dead. Can't get it started."

"Jeez, that's a riot," Buddy mumbled as his guffaw roared into high gear. He couldn't stop laughing even as I tried to impress him with the seriousness of my predicament. "I can get some rags and help you dry off the engine," he eventually was able to say, between great guffaws.

The idea appealed to me. From his back shed we gathered up a bunch of rags and we both retuned to the taxi. He watched as I rubbed the rags over the top of the engine, carefully wiped down each of the sparkplug wires, and dabbed a dry rag on top of the battery to collect the standing wet residue. I looked up and saw that Buddy had written "help me" with his finger on the salt spray that collected on the windshield. I threw him a clean rag.

"Wipe that shit off," I yelled. Buddy thought it hilarious but proceeded to wipe the windshield clean.

"Let's try to get it started," I said as much to myself as to Buddy. "If it starts, slam down the hood right away cause I got to get down to the Pines as soon as I can." I got in the driver's seat. The engine kicked over a few times but soon died. I couldn't keep it running.

"Keep trying," Buddy encouraged me as he peered into the engine compartment. No luck. Soon even the battery gave out.

Buddy and I sat together on the tailgate at the rear of the jeep as I tried to conjure up what might be a solution.

"I know, "Buddy blurted out. "You steer and I'll push

you down to the Pines."

"That's a stupid idea. You can't be serious," I told Buddy. One never knew what Buddy thought was possible.

"Does your father have an extra battery on the boat?" I asked Buddy.

"Probably."

"Well let's go get it."

"Can't."

"Why not?

"Cause the boat's not here. Neither is my father."

"Crap," was all I could muster up in response.

We sat silently for a few minutes on the tailgate. No more insights came bursting through, not even stupid ones. My blank stare suddenly focused on a distant vehicle approaching from the east along the beach. When it drew closer, clearly I could see it was a red jeep with a white top - a White Cap taxi.

"That's gotta be Everett," I yelled out.

"So?" Buddy responded.

"He's gonna have my ass when he sees I'm stuck here."

"Well let's get out of here, Buddy said. "Let's run over the dunes before he gets here."

"That's even stupider than pushing the jeep. " Buddy never quite had the ability to grasp the finer meaning of awkward circumstances. "He knows it's my taxi. He's not gonna just drive by."

"But if he doesn't see us here, maybe he'll think you're at your house having lunch or something and just drive by," Buddy said.

"I just left him an hour ago," I replied. "He knows my jeep. And he knows I'm supposed to be at the Pines. Of course he will stop."

"You're toast," Buddy said. "You want me hanging around?"

"Probably not. He might think you're the reason I stopped." Buddy hustled down the beach, up the stairs, and over the dunes. I could still see his head poking out between blades of beach grass. Hide and seek was not one of his strong suits.

"This is crap," I thought to myself. "He'll probably fire my ass on the spot." I thought again about excuses, but no probable explanation seemed appropriate for why I was sitting on the tailgate with a dead engine when I was expected at Fire Island Pines. Salt spray all over the cab was a dead giveaway. I was sure he wouldn't buy any plausible explanation like I stopped to deliver a message for Buddy's father or to check to see the condition of our house after the long winter and when I tried to restart the engine, the battery was already dead. That would not explain why the jeep had salt spray all over it.

Moments later Everett's taxi pulled up alongside. Without getting out of his cab, he asked "What's up? Why are you sitting here?" I could see a distinct glare in his eyes hinting of his rising suspicion.

"Got a slight problem," I explained. "The engine quit on me and the battery is dead." I used my most relaxed voice, but still felt the churning inside my gut. I half expected him to immediately blurt out "You're fired. Go home. You're an idiot."

"You think the battery is dead. What do you mean you think?" were his exact words. "And that don't explain why you got salt spray all over the cab." Buddy had at least wiped the "help me" sign off the windshield.

I had no response. I felt compelled not to reveal any more information than absolutely necessary. I thought it best to keep quiet. The circumstances were out of my control. I was ready to accept whatever resolution happened. Not saying anything seemed my best option.

Everett got out of his cab and walked over to my taxi. The hood was already open. He stuck his head inside the engine compartment. "Hit a wave, didn't you?"

"Yeah, that happened," I said. "Just sorta came up from nowhere."

"Water doesn't get all over the cab from nowhere," Everett replied. "I told you about driving too close to the surf." He continued inspecting the taxi in silence, looking again into the engine compartment, and then walking around the cab wiping his fingers across the salt spray as if dusting the living room furniture. He wasn't talking. I wished he had said something so I could gauge his attitude and my chances for survival.

Keeping to my policy of damage control, I offered no excuses. I stood back away from the jeep and just watched Everett. I got caught and could now only wait for the consequences. I was expecting the worse. "You're fired" were the next words I expected out of Everett's mouth.

Everett said nothing while I watched him get back into his jeep, start his engine, and slowly pull his front bumper up close until it was adjacent to my front bumper. Nose to nose the two taxis sat. He then took jumper cables out from behind his back seat, attached one end to his battery, and then the other end to my battery. He took the top off my carburetor and sprayed some aerosol concoction into it. He quickly replaced the top of the carburetor.

"Get in your jeep," he instructed me. "When I tell you, try to start it, but don't give it a lot of gas." He got back into his jeep, revved his engine, and yelled, "Now, start it now."

I turned the ignition on, and almost immediately the engine let out an immense roar. I let back on the gas and it settled into a smooth idle. Everett detached the cables and returned to his own cab.

Through the window of his taxi, Everett yelled, "Get going, and don't screw up again." With that said, he turned his jeep around and headed back down the beach in the direction from which he came.

Buddy, who had watched the whole episode from his perch atop the dunes, sidled back down to the beach. "Do you think someone told him you were stuck?" he asked.

"Like who? We don't have a working phone here and nobody else has come past." I said.

"Jeez," Buddy said. "He must be a mind reader or maybe he's got, what do you call it, mental telephoning."

"Mental telepathy," I said, "and no, I don't think so." Buddy thought that was hilarious and broke into a hearty laugh. *Mental telephony*, I thought, *how stupid can you be?* I could still hear Buddy laughing as I drove off toward Fire Island Pines.

7

Roger's Office

Personnel Officer: *So what is it? Why do you want to*
  be a taxi driver?
  Do you need a second job? Are you moonlighting?
Travis Bickle: *I... I just want to work long hours.*
  What's moonlighting?

  --*Taxi* (the movie) 1976

Fire Island Pines, one of the notable gay communities
on the island, was accessible to taxis from the beach front
through a cut in the dunes. I could drive directly into the
community. I pulled my jeep up next to the other White
Cap taxis I saw parked alongside the harbor near the ferry
landing. It was an exquisite harbor that extended inland
about a quarter mile or so. Fifty or more pleasure boats where
tied up alongside. The ferry landing was at the near end of
the harbor. A restaurant and a few boutiques surrounded the
perimeter of the harbor. Guys in tee shirts and baseball caps
sat on the tailgates of the taxis. I wasn't exactly sure where
I needed to park my cab so parked it alongside the others. I
wandered over and asked one of them if they knew where
I could find Roger.

"Why? Is he lost?" one of the guys replied. They all
laughed at his wittiness.

"I'm going to be driving for him and I need to check in. Just tell me where he might be." I tried not to show any annoyance at their response. One of them pointed to a small brown-shingled building about a hundred yards from the dock. As I walked away, I could hear snippets like, "He must be a new guy. He don't know jack shit yet."

"The office is around the back," one of them yelled as I was walking away. "Roger should be there." A boardwalk led around the back of the building to a door that opened into a small room about the size of a large closet. Inside was a very large man sitting on the bottom bunk eating a sandwich. He was so big he had to lean forward so as not to bang his head on the top bunk. There seemed hardly room for anyone else in the office. He was dressed in brown khaki head to toe, the same Nazi color that Everett wore. My suspicion was that he must be Roger, the other partner. I could see stains on his shirt, on his pants, and grease on the side of his face. When I looked in, he looked up at me.

"What can I do you for?" he said. His voice mumbled. I figured it was the ham sandwich interfering.

"You must be Roger," I said. "Everett Wright sent me down here from Davis Park. I'm Peter. I'm supposed to be driving for you."

He took another bite of his sandwich. "I hear you already got stuck just trying to get here. Driving too close to the surf will get you every time." He thought that was hilarious and began a belly laugh that ended with his coughing as he started to choke on his sandwich. He reached for a bottle of water sitting on a chair beside him, drank from it, took a moment to regain his composure, and stood up. He was many inches taller than six feet. He wiped his hands on his shirt and stuck one hand out to me. "Glad to meet you. I'm Roger." He had huge hands. When I shook his hand, it felt like I was holding a freshly oiled baseball glove.

Roger and Everett located themselves at different parts of the Island. Everett worked from Davis Park east of the Pines and supplemented the taxi service income with his work at the Davis Park Casino. I eventually learned that Roger was in charge of the daily operations from the small office at Fire Island Pines. Most of the customer service emanated from here. Neither of the two spent much time at the other location.

Roger invited me into the office. It was either actually small or his large presence made it feel small. There seemed barely room enough for the two of us to squeeze in. A bunk bed was wedged against one wall and a table against the other wall. One small chair stood by itself in the middle of the room which I had to circumnavigate in order for me to get inside the office. Barebones was the best way to describe the furnishings; nothing ostentatious here.

"This is my office. Yeah, it's small," he said as he sat back down on the lower bunk and leaned his head forward again to avoid the top bunk. "We need a dispatcher, someone to stay here and answer the phone. Don't have one now, so I got to do it sometimes." On the table was an elaborate looking radio, I guessed it was a radio because it looked like one except that it had a lot more dials on it than any radio I had seen before. A curled cord led from the back of the apparatus to a microphone that lay next to the radio.

"This here is the base set," he said pointing to the radio. "When we get calls or I need to talk to one of the drivers, I call you on this here radio and you answer with the one in your cab. You got to keep your radio on and no jabbering about other stuff." I presumed that he meant it was for taxi business only, not personal conversations. "Until we get a dispatcher, I can't be in here all the time so we're gonna take turns, you and the other drivers, being here and answering the phone. You gotta do it when it's your turn." I told him that was fine.

"Do you know how to get to Ocean Beach or down to the Grove?" he asked.

"I think so."

"When people call and want a taxi, they want to be picked up at certain walks. You gotta learn which walk is which, or you'll be sitting at one place and they will be at another place and then they call back and yell at me cause the taxi ain't there. That's no good. So you gotta learn these walks as quick as you can." Roger looked up at me as if he needed to say something else, but didn't. He just stared. "Did you get all that?' is what I assumed he meant to say. "I think I got it," I replied.

"You go to college or something?" he asked. I wasn't expecting that question. I was concentrating on the instructions he just told me.

"Uh...yeah, sort of. I'm in college during the winter but not now."

"We got other college kids driving," Roger continued. I think he would have continued whether I said I was in college or not. He wanted to make a point. "And geez, you'd think they was smart, but they're the ones that screw up the most. They can't seem to get things right. I hope you're a smarter college kid than that."

"Well I'm pretty good at learning things," I told him. I couldn't tell if he seriously thought college students were dumb, or if he was just baiting me, looking for a response. I was afraid to ask if he went to college. It might have sounded like an affront.

"I got to get something else to eat," Roger changed the subject, probably because he didn't get an interesting response from me about college students. "This sandwich ain't enough. I'm still growing, you know." A hearty belly laugh ensued. "You stay in the office while I'm gone."

"You want me to stay here? What do you want me to do if someone calls?"

"Answer it. You're a college kid. You can figure it out." With that, he disappeared out the door.

Less than five minutes later the phone rang. "White Cap Taxi," I said. I listened intently to a request for a pick up at six o'clock at Sunset Walk at Ocean Beach. He wanted to go to the Grove. He ended the request with a strong admonition. "You're sure you'll have the taxi there at that time, right?"

"Uh...yeah, of course," I said. "Let me write this down. Sunset walk...six o'clock...Ocean Beach," I repeated what he said.

"And the name is Brooks, Mel Brooks."

"Got it, Brooks...Sunset walk....six o'clock...Ocean Beach," I repeated one more time. He hung up.

"Damn," I thought to myself. "That sounds familiar. Mel Brooks. No, it couldn't be. It was that raspy voice that I thought I recognized. I was sure I had heard it before. But I was more intent on getting the information correct than trying to remember names.

Talking on a phone felt strange. I was not used to phones at the beach. Giving up phone use was part of the tradition when coming to the beach. Water Island had one phone and it was a recent addition. It was installed in a glass phone booth at the end of the last boardwalk to the west. It was a pay phone and took only correct change. Since most of the residents wore only bathing suits most of the day and into the evening, there was no place to hold a pocketful of nickels, dimes, or quarters. Any call from the island was a long distance call, and required a wheel-barrow full of correct change just to call the grocery store. Consequently, the phone got little use. Besides, it always seemed to be out of service just when you wanted to use it. Frequently it was the phone that didn't work, but more often it was the booth itself that needed maintenance. During the winter months, when rain and salt air covered the phone booth, rust would accumulate. The early arriving residents, the ones who lived just across the bay and had their own boats, usually took responsibility for oiling the door so people could get into the booth. Sometimes they forgot this task, and entering the phone booth became an obstacle. We took the door off its hinges to gain access.

At Fire Island Pines, the community developer installed electricity and phone service. There were pay phones conveniently placed but rarely used. The objective on the island was to avoid outside contact unless absolutely necessary. The taxi office had electric lights and a phone. They looked like they belonged, part of the décor, as if they had always been there. Still, for me, talking on a telephone in an electrically lighted room while at the beach felt incongruent, as if I they were for show and not functional.

I didn't want to disappoint Mr. Brooks. I certainly didn't relish having to tell Roger that a smart college student couldn't get a phone message straight. I was determined to get this call out to one of the drivers. Figuring out how to use the base radio couldn't be that hard even though Roger hadn't instructed me on its use. "I can figure this out. I'm a college student," I assured myself.

I looked at the menagerie of knobs on the base set. Each was identified by a label—volume, range, squelch, and frequency. These were functions with which I wasn't familiar, but they were not altogether alien. I remembered reading about them in high school physics. "I'll turn up the volume," I thought. "I need to hear well." I left the others alone. I noticed a little light on the side of the base set. It glared red. I pushed the microphone button in and the light turned green. "Green means go," I thought. "I must be doing something right."

"Hello, anybody out there?" I said. Nobody answered. I tried again while still holding down the button "Hey. Anybody hear me? I got a call for a fare." I waited. No response. I waited another fifteen seconds making sure the green light was always on next to the microphone. I called once more. "We have a fare down at Ocean Beach. Can someone pick this person up? Please let me know." I repeated. I waited some more. I then put the microphone down on the table and started to turn some of the dials with the hope that it might come alive with voices. Just at that moment, one of the drivers whom I recognized sitting on the cab tailgate outside the office when I first arrived, poked his head in the door.

"You have to let go of the talk button on the mic if you want anyone to respond," he said. "Either that or stick your head out the door and tell one of us. We're all just sitting here. I'm Terry, by the way, and I can take the call."

"Oh...Yeah, I forgot," I said. I didn't know any better but wanted to appear more aware than I was feeling. "Nice to meet you Terry." I looked at the paper where I wrote down the information. "It's at Sunset Walk at Ocean Beach," I told him.

"Yeah, I heard it half a dozen times. It's Mr. Brooks, right?" he said.

"Do you know him?" I asked

"Not personally, but everybody knows who Mel Brooks is," He replied.

It suddenly dawned on me. Mel Brooks, Carl Reiner, Sid Caesar. *The Show of Shows.* Saturday night television. My mother made us eat TV dinners on Saturday night just so she could watch the *Show of Shows.* My father nearly choked to death with laughter when Mel Brooks did his two-thousand-year-old man routine. It was the same Mel Brooks.

Roger returned with another huge sandwich. With his mouth full, he muttered, "Got any calls?"

"Got one," I said. "Terry said he could get it." I didn't offer to tell Roger about the fiasco I encountered with the base radio. "A guy named Mel Brooks at Ocean Beach wanted to go to Cherry Grove. Is that the same Mel Brooks who's on television?"

"You get to drive a lot of actors and television people out here. They like to come down to the Grove at night, especially Saturday nights. I've driven Mel Brooks myself. One time with Anne Bancroft," he said. I didn't immediately make the connection, but from the way Roger included her, I suspected she was an impressive celebrity.

Roger's temperament seemed more suited than Everett's did for working with the drivers. He was gregarious and seemed at ease joking with the hired hands. Although Roger had the reputation for having a temper, it wasn't obvious from his friendly welcome.

As the summer progressed, I sometimes felt uncomfortable talking with him, as if I was intruding on his time, which he would rather be spending doing something else. But Roger liked to talk. He took an interest in the drivers. Almost without fail, each time we took off from the office for a pickup, Roger would ask, "You gotta nuffa gas?" I interpreted that as an expression of caring. Others thought it more his questioning our responsibility. "If you don't have "nuffa" gas, make sure you put some in because I don't want to have to come and bring you any."

For the rest of that evening, I stayed in the office. Roger wandered in and out. When he was in he sat on the bottom bunk and asked questions. "Why you want to drive a taxi?

How long have you lived at Water Island? What college you go to? How much does college cost you? So you're related to Harvey Shand." There wasn't enough room for the two of us, so I sat in the chair which I moved just outside the door. Only a few times did the phone ring and Roger was there each time. I watched how he used the base radio to call out fares.

"Pick up at Pat's Place," he said into the microphone. Then he let the button up. Immediately a response came back.

"Got it."

"Who's that?"

"It's me, Frank," Roger seemed satisfied and nothing else was said.

When Frank returned to the Pines with his fare, he stopped into the office. He said he was hungry, needed a snack and had to take a pee, in that order. I think he also wanted to see the novice driver who didn't know how to use the base radio. Before he left, he offered some tidbits of information.

"Don't cross Roger," was his first bit of advice. "He can get mean, and he's big enough where it can make a difference. Last summer he caught one of the drivers holding back on the money split and I saw him literally pick the guy off the ground and throw him off the boardwalk, right here, right outside the door." I made a mental note of that. It also gave me a chance to question how drivers were paid.

"Every Monday you and Roger sit down, count your fares and then split the money sixty/forty; sixty percent for the taxi company and forty percent for you," Frank explained. "And don't try to hold back any cause Roger's got a way of knowing and gets really pissed if he thinks someone is holding back."

Without my asking, Frank had more advice. "Sometimes you get some horny chicks in your cab," he said. "I can show you some nice places up behind the dunes where nobody can see the cab." I listened to all the advice he had to offer. "Stay away from Sonny. He's harmless but a real bullshitter. He likes to hustle away our fares. Sometimes the Boatell Restaurant will give you free food, but you got to go around back. Straight drunks from up at Ocean Beach or Ocean Bay Park tip better than sober queers do. These fairies are really tight with their money." I thanked Frank for the advice. It was more information than I could assimilate at one time. I would have to sort it out later.

Nothing was said by Roger or the other drivers who stopped by that evening about working hours. I didn't feel comfortable enough to ask but wondered what time I was expected to come to work and what time work was over. I was used to jobs that had specific hours, usually 9:00 – 5:00, five days a week.

Eight-thirty came and went, and I was still in the office. Roger vacillated in and out saying that he needed to fix something whenever he left. He'd be gone a few minutes and then return looking dirty. No one mentioned anything about quitting time. Ten-thirty came and went. Nothing changed. It was now after midnight. Calls were few, hardly enough to keep two drivers busy. I used the time to listen to talk on the base set. Despite that Roger insisted drivers not use the radios for idle chatter, there was constant banter about queers approaching the taxis, about "splendid" chics that were off limits because they were "lezzies, and the latest nudes from this month's Playboy magazine. Whenever Roger was present, he'd immediately chine in on the radio, "I told you guys, no chatter." The drivers had a sixth sense about knowing that Roger would leave again, and the "chatter" continued.

I tried to remember where certain walks were when I heard a driver say where he was going. I impressed even myself with the diligence I paid to learning a new job. Roger had taken a few calls himself in his own cab. He returned to the office about twelve-thirty. I wasn't sure if Roger spent the night right there in the office.

I was feeling some anxiety, wondering how much longer before I got to leave. I didn't ask Roger but he volunteered. "Why don't you leave now?" he said. "Things are pretty quiet tonight. Frank and Terry are still out there. Most of the nights we don't get done till the bars close."

"When's that?"

"Bout two or three."

As I left the office, Roger told me to be back before noon the next day. He said he would show me about gassing up and where to get spare tires. "You're gonna have lots of flats from boards with nails in them." Some people don't like cabs on the beach and they try to sabotage us. And stay out of the ocean."

I had no trouble starting my jeep this time. I felt confident I could keep it going until I reached Davis Park. I did drive cautiously along the beach, constantly on the lookout for the boards with nails in them and a sufficient distance away from the breaking waves. I reached Davis Park without incident and parked the jeep where I had picked it up earlier that day. My adrenalin was still flowing too fast to go to bed. I knew I couldn't sleep yet. I sat on Aunt Ethel's steps and drank a beer. I was having mixed feelings. The idea of driving on the beach for the summer still intrigued me, but the working hours -- it sounded like fifteen hours each day -- caused me some distress. Could I manage it? I went to bed that night hoping I would have a clearer perspective in the morning. My first day of the ideal summer job was now complete. Maybe it wasn't as ideal as I first imagined.

8

"The Fog Creeps in on Little Cat Feet"

There's a woman I see who's not my therapist, but she's like an old friend who's a therapist in profession. She lets me talk to her like a therapist once in a while, and she does a great thing. Whenever I have a big dilemma, like this is a big problem in my life, she always says, 'Wow, you're going to have to figure that out.'
— Louis C.K.

Parking a car is usually a simple matter. It shouldn't present major obstacles, unless one lives in a metropolitan area. In New York City, often the only place to park is third in line from the curb (triple parking) which is an open invitation for the parking meter lady to bring on the tow truck. An alternative is to contract with a private parking garage. You pay an exorbitant rate and then still have to trudge the ten blocks to your apartment. Either way, parking presents one of the greatest hazards for the car owner in an urban setting. Having lived in or near cities most of my driving life, I was becoming used to these perils.

Fire Island provided a pleasant parking reprieve from the hassles of city life. Finding space to park the jeep was not an obstacle; it was a no-brainer. Since there were no roads, there were no parking restrictions, and no other vehicles to provide hindrances. The beach was wide open territory. That's what I assumed, but I was wrong. It wasn't for the lack of space or crowded conditions or restrictions of any kind that parking proved an aggravation. It was the weather.

Beachfronts were notorious for being clammy. Locals liked to refer to this condition as heavy humidity, but damp and soggy was a much more accurate description. The breaking ocean waves constantly saturated the surrounding air with moisture as if a giant had rung out a wet dishcloth and the early morning hours produced a fog-like environment. Carl Sandberg wrote of fog creeping *in on little cat feet. It sits on silent haunches, looking over harbor and city,* but what it really does is eat away the innards of any metal obstacle lying dormant in its midst, particularly vehicles left standing on the beach.

Years before there existed a cut at Water Island, a way to drive inside the dunes and off the beach front. When winter storms eroded the sand and collapsed the dunes, the Army Corps of Engineers hauled in heavy dredging equipment and, with an action similar to a giant vacuum cleaner, sucked up sand offshore and deposited it where the dunes used to be. With the protective dunes restored, well-meaning local folk with an eye toward environmental improvement and property protection planted beach grass on the top and sides of the new dunes for erosion control.

For beachfront homeowners, protecting sand dunes bordered on the sacred. Signs placed nearby warned of dire consequences for tramping on the dunes. To step foot upon these revered surroundings was to invoke the extreme ire of the foreboding dune god who, for the slightest infraction of the rules, would fill your swim shorts with heavy wet sand. "Stay off the dunes" was more than a warning; it was a threat, a mandate strictly enforced by well-intentioned, but unforgiving residents. Out of respect, or perhaps fear, I dared not think of driving over the dunes to access our house at Water Island. So I parked the taxi on the beachfront, exposed to the extreme elements.

"Why don't you stay at Ethel's house?" Everett questioned me each time I ran into him those first weeks. "You'll be inside the dunes."

"I can't. She already has other company."

"If you leave your cab on the beach, it'll be a bitch to start in the morning," was his retort. This conversation repeated itself each time I happened to see Everett. So far I had no problems starting the jeep in the morning.

One day Everett resorted to a different strategy. It was show and tell time. He pulled an old blanket out from behind the front seat of his jeep. "Cover the engine with this at night," he told me.

He held the blanket up for me to see. At first I thought he was joking, jerking me around because of my reluctance to take his advice about staying at Aunt Ethel's. I figured he was having fun harassing the new guy, sort of like the proverbial snipe hunt. I was skeptical. It sounded like I was going to put my baby sister to bed and tuck her in under the blankie.

Everett appeared serious. "It will keep the engine warmer and keep the salt air off," he said.

"Won't it catch on fire?" I asked pretending to sound innocent as if I was playing along with the joke.

"You don't put the blanket right on the engine," he said. "You throw it over the front hood." He then threw it over the front hood of my taxi as a demonstration. "Just leave it like that overnight." Everett was dead serious.

I took the blanket. I felt like I couldn't refuse. It remained unused in the back of my jeep.

Roger, the other taxi owner, also didn't like that I parked on the beach at night, but for a different reason.

"If I got to get up and come down there to get you started, it's gonna piss me off," he told me. Roger didn't mince words. "I get grumpy in the morning." He then let out a hearty laugh. I was never sure, when following one of his mandates, whether he was laughing at me or that he thought what he said was extremely funny.

It was a particularly foggy morning. A front had moved in from the east during the night, bringing light rain and heavy winds. Driven by the wind, the ocean waves lapped higher up on the beach, giving off a wisp of constant spray. In the morning when I approached the jeep, I immediately noticed the accumulation of salt spray. It lay thick as a blanket over the whole jeep. I wondered about the engine. I hadn't used Everett's blanket therapy.

"Shit," I thought to myself. First priority was starting the engine. If I got the engine started, I could use the windshield wipers to clear the windshield. I immediately inserted the key in the ignition. The engine cranked over and over, but didn't fire up. Lots of chugging noises, but no spark, no roar. I had so hoped to hear that roar.

"It's got to be wet spark plugs," I thought.

I searched for a dry rag in the back of the cab, but most of them felt damp. I reached further down and under the pile of rags I found a clean one that hadn't been as exposed to the humidity.

"Come on rag, be my salvation," I mumbled to myself.

When I opened the hood, water droplets were everywhere. Water formed in small pools on top of the engine block, having dripped off spark plug wires. I wiped the wires until they felt dry, or at least drier. I wiped the battery terminals. Everything looked dry.

I got back in the cab and attempted to start the engine. I could hear the rrr, rrr, rrr of the starter motor. Still no spark and no roar. I kept the starter motor going full tilt, but it failed to start the engine. Soon, even the starter motor slowed to barely a hum, a sure sign the battery was dying.

I recognized I had a grave dilemma. I had to save a bit of battery juice to run the radio, otherwise, I would not have access to call Roger to come and relieve me of my predicament. The thought of arousing his ire, however, convinced me that it might be better to sit and wait a few minutes and try to start the engine on my own. The sun was not breaking through the clouds and the dampness seemed to hang on forever, so I sat for a while and sorted out my options.

"There has got to be a way to get this heap going," I thought to myself. Since my first encounter with Everett after hitting a wave and the subsequent threats by both Roger and Everett about the consequences of parking on the beach, I wasn't looking forward to a bailout. Panic began to set in, but reason won out, however, and I decided to use the remaining battery power to call Roger on the radio for suggestions. There might be a simple solution if I sounded composed.

"I need to talk to Roger," I said to the voice who answered.

"Not now," he replied. "He's eating his breakfast and doesn't want to talk with anyone." Very close behind rule No.1 – never try to cheat Roger out of his cut of the taxi fares – was rule No.2. Never disturb Roger when he is eating. He gets really, really grumpy. I recalled the words of my Aunt Ethel: "Roger was a big man and known for his temper."

My dilemma demanded I take a chance. "Tell him I can't get my damn jeep started. The battery's dead. I'm down at Water Island."

"That's gonna piss him off right now,"

"You got any better suggestions?"

"Nope, but as soon as I tell him, I'm outa here." There was an uneasy silence for a moment, and then in the background I heard swearing and cursing. Then silence again. I kept the radio on, but with the talk button off to reserve battery power. While I waited for Roger, I started processing possible excuses. "It rained so hard last night, it blew in sideways." That sounded lame since there was only a slight drizzle. "Someone tried to steal the taxi and left the hood up after they tried hot-wiring it." That was an even worse excuse, totally unbelievable even for someone as gullible as Roger was.

Roger came over the radio in a voice so loud that I might not have needed a radio to hear him.

"You can't get it started?" he bellowed. "What do you mean you can't get it started?" In addition to the volume, there was also a mumbling noise that sounded like he was still eating. Roger had a habit of repeating what you just said to him before advancing the conversation. People who repeat the obvious, who say again to you what you just said to them, always bothered me. If I said, "Can I have a hamburger?" and they say in reply, "Can you have a hamburger? Sure you can," The impression I get is they didn't understand the meaning of what I said, or they wanted to correct what I said, or they were wondering if I even knew what a hamburger was.

There was silence on the radio for a few moments while I heard Roger talking with someone in the background. "Do you have any WD-40 in your jeep?" he asked in a more subdued tone.

"What's that?"

"WD-40," he replied. His voice was rising in volume again. "A can of WD-40. It's that oil spray."

"I'll look. Hang on a second." I was not familiar with WD-40, but figured if there was a can of it somewhere in the taxi, that I could identify it by the name. Lo and behold, under the back seat was a can. "Yeah, I got some WD-40.".

"You got some WD-40?" Roger repeated. "Spray it on the spark plug wires. Do you know what the spark plug wires look like?" Roger was already convinced that I was an idiot after only a few weeks.

"How much should I spray?"

"A lot," A lot was an amount that sounded a bit ambiguous, but I didn't want to press the issue.

I shut down the radio in an effort to save battery power. WD-40 came in an aerosol spray about the size of a coke can. I pointed the tip toward the wires and pressed the top. I continued spraying until the can felt light, as if almost empty. The wires, as well as the top of the engine, dripped with oil. "Guess that's a lot," I muttered to myself.

Back in the cab, I turned the ignition key to on to start the engine. At the same time I pressed the accelerator pedal down to release gas to the engine. Swoosh. A billow of smoke suddenly burst from the engine compartment, and then flames appeared.

"Oh shit. What now?" was my knee jerk reaction. It took a few seconds of surprised staring before I could function. The engine was on fire. "Put the damn fire out, but how?" I thought.

I jumped out of the cab in fear the entire taxi might soon explode in one large fire-ball. Instinctively I reached down, grabbed a handful of sand, and threw it onto the engine, then another handful and another after that. After a few more handfuls of sand, the fire subsided. As the smoke cleared, I cautiously peered under the hood, still a bit apprehensive the flames might flare up again. No smoke. No flames. The fire was out but sand still covered the top of the engine. I wanted to assess the damage, but didn't really know what I was looking for. I gave up the investigation.

I dreaded my next radio call to Roger. I hoped there was no permanent damage to the engine and that Roger might have a simple solution. Any excuse I might offer for burning up his taxi would sound feeble unless I could convince him it happened as a consequence of what he told me to do. "But Roger, you told me to spray lots of WD-40 on the wires. I did that." I rehearsed my explanation. Any explanation would sound more feasible if it was prefaced by "But you told me to do that, Roger."

With my heart beating wildly, I turned on the radio. It still had power. "It's me again, Peter," I said to the driver who answered in the office. "I need to talk to Roger again."

"He's outside changing out a gas tank. Someone put sand in the tank. You really don't want to talk with him right now. He's in a foul mood."

"Things aren't going well here either," I told him. "As soon as he's done, tell him I'm stuck at Water Island. My engine caught on fire."

Sand in a gas tank. What a coincidence. And I got sand all over the engine. I sat for a while in the cab thinking, then got out and walked around a bit, still thinking, and then sat on the tailgate doing some more thinking. All that thinking was unproductive except to give me a headache. I gave up thinking and radioed the office again. Roger answered.

When I heard his voice, I prepared myself for some abusive cursing and yelling and his reiteration about how stupid college kids can be with all that learning. Instead, I heard this hearty belly laugh and then the words, "I bet that scared the shit out of you." Then another round of guffaws. All the while all the other drivers with radios on were hearing his comments.

One hour later, Roger pulled up beside me in his big International Harvester station wagon. Without a word, he went straight toward my opened hood and peered in. "Holy shit. What did you do here? Looks like a hurricane blew through. There's sand everywhere," he said in a nonchalant manner.

"I had to put the fire out," I replied.

"What fire?"

"It caught fire after I did what you told me to do. You know, spray WD-40 on the wires." I guessed the driver I spoke with forgot to mention anything about the fire or Roger forgot, which he often did, what I told him an hour beforehand.

"How much WD-40 did you use?"

I held up the empty can. "Most of it," I said.

"Most of it." Roger repeated every word I said. "Jesus, you're lucky you didn't burn the whole cab. That would have been something, huh."

"Yeah. That would have been something," I repeated.

It took Roger only a few minutes to wipe and blow away much of the sand that had accumulated on the top of the engine and then fiddle with some wires, which ones I didn't observe, as I stayed a safe distance away until he said, "Okay, get in and see if we can get it started."

The engine roared to a start almost immediately. No flames appeared and no smoke billowed up.

"You only have been here a couple of weeks," he said to me as he proceeded to get back in his International. "You sure have been a pain in the ass." He turned away from me and started to laugh. It was at that moment that I realized that the opinions about Roger I had formed from listening to Aunt Ethel were overblown. His bark was worse than his bite. From that experience I quickly learned to trust my can of WD-40, but with greater moderation. I never did learn to use Everett's blanket therapy.

9

Taxi Etiquette

*Before they're plumbers or writers or taxi drivers or
unemployed or journalists, before everything else, men
are men. Whether heterosexual, or homosexual. The only
difference is that some of them remind you of it as soon
as you meet them, and others wait a little while.*

--Marquerite Duras

Vehicles have always been present on Fire Island. As far
back as anyone can remember, people had been bringing
old Model T's across to the Island on barges. Because these
vintage autos had huge fly-wheels and a low gear ratio,
they provided good traction on the soft beach sand when
equipped with oversized balloon tires. The county engineers
constructed a bridge at Smith Point near the far eastern
end of the island. After that, most commercial businesses
accessed the island with newer four-wheel-drive vehicles
which they used to deliver goods and services to residents –
plumbers, carpenters, and laundry suppliers.

White Cap Taxi Company was born out of necessity. As the
island swelled with population and the construction of new
housing during the late 50's, the demand for transportation
services escalated beyond anyone's imagination. Taxis on the

beach front operated more quickly, more conveniently, and for less money than any type of ferryboat service between island communities. Soon, Everett and Roger had a dozen taxis operating during the summer season. Communities once isolated from each other no longer felt disconnected. People moved about. The gay bars and clubs at Cherry Grove and Fire Island Pines became accessible to the party-craving straight crowd who had an insatiable curiosity about this growing avant-garde phenomenon. Although the straights chose to live in more traditional communities, the intrigue of the queer culture fascinated them. Thus began the constant flow of the night time population bent on satisfying their inquisitiveness about the lure of the gay community and specifically the mysterious intrigue that characterized Cherry Grove and Fire Island Pines. The little red wagons, once representative of the chosen isolation went the way of the Model T. Staying put in one place no longer was sufficient. People began to venture out of their home communities. Business was booming for White Cap Taxi.

As a taxi driver, I quickly recognized that I needed to know the new traffic flow patterns that emerged from this constant need to explore. If I were to be successful and benefit from my resolve to make the summer months as profitable as possible, in addition to being just a beach bum, I needed to know where people wanted to go and when they wanted to be there. I was glad the summer sun had not completely fried my brain and recognized that the entrepreneurial bug had bitten me sufficiently. To maximize efficiency and profitability, I needed to be in the right place at the right time. I needed a calculated plan.

In the early evening, for instance, I learned people focused on finding restaurants. From both ends of the Island, people sought to migrate toward the middle, toward Cherry Grove and Fire Island Pines, where most of the more intriguing bistros were located. These places acted like magnets and not simply because of their menus. Those wishing to experience or just observe gay lives were attracted there en masse. Saturday night was "show time" at Cherry Grove.

The businesses at Cherry Grove and Fire Island Pines were most accommodating to the ever-increasing straight crowd. Particularly on weekends, these people fueled the restaurant and bar business at both Cherry Grove and Fire Island Pines. A symbiotic arrangement existed between these businesses and taxi drivers. We both benefited. Curiosity reigned supreme. Visiting straights wishing to join the frivolity of the gay life-style became our primary source of revenue. The bars and clubs acted as magnets, creating a need for transportation. The taxis obliged with more and more patrons for these businesses. We fed off each other. It was a workable arrangement and profitable for both of us.

On Saturday nights, taxi traffic was unrelenting. It resembled a military convoy. A steady stream of similar looking vehicles followed in virtual straight lines back and forth up and down the beach front like ducklings following their mother. Between 5:00 P.M. and 9:00 P.M., everybody wanted to go to the Grove or the Pines. I made it my routine to be always somewhere in route, either on my way to the Grove or coming back from it. It was a shuttle service. I could always count on filling the cab to the maximum. Being anywhere else during those hours meant a significant loss of customers and cash.

Attempting to reserve a taxi on a Saturday night was like waiting for the cable guy to show up. It just wasn't going to happen. Drivers largely ignored people who made reservations. There was enough business just by being present on the beach with the motor running. Waiting in one spot for a reservation to show up was a waste of time. Many an angry customer would make a return call to Roger complaining that no cab showed up when requested, and eventually even Roger grew to ignore these requests on weekend evenings.

The people we brought down to the Grove or the Pines expected us to transport them home again later that evening or early in the morning after the bars closed. The process of shuttling began once again in earnest just after 1:00 A.M and usually wasn't completed until well past 3:00 A.M. Late night taxis lined up at the Grove at the bottom of the main boardwalk leading to the beach. Thus began the nightly ritual of drunks stumbling down the steps and onto the beach expecting a taxi to be present. Rarely did they appear without a drink in hand – gin and tonic – and rarely did they make it to the bottom step without spilling the entire beverage. Their clothes reeked of alcohol as much as their breaths. Each person or group was hustled into the first cab in line. We filled each cab to capacity, up to ten or more people, and took off.

Once delivered to their destination, it was always tempting to over charge them, a real lure since they could hardly remember their names, much less how much the ride costs. Many of these late night patrons forget where they came from and counted on the drivers to remember. I can't guarantee that we always brought people back to the right place. Surprisingly, and I speak for myself alone, I resisted this enticement. The exception, of course, was if the passenger was female, drunk, and flaunting her availability, Not that I would ever imagine taking advantage of someone because they were inebriated, but if initiated by that person, who was I to protest. There were some circumstances that always took priority over making money.

Once I delivered my fares, I quickly returned to take my place again at the bottom of the steps in the dispatching line. Little protocol was given to returning customers. We pushed people into each cab helter skelter, wherever and however one more body could fit. The customer's state of inebriation made this workable.

Particularly on weekend nights, drivers stubbornly avoided certain locations, while others were preferred. Davis Park was one area studiously avoided on a week-end night. Calls would come into the office and the dispatcher Paul, would radio to all cabs.

"There's a pick up for 8:00 at Jones Walk in Davis Park. Who's got it?"

Silence.

"Come on guys," he would repeat. "Davis Park pickup at 8:00. They called."

Again silence.

Frustrated, and almost frantic, Paul would plead with the drivers. "Please, I told these people we would pick them up. They are probably waiting on the beach right now. Who's going take this call?"

Still no answer.

No one responded because going to Davis Park on a weekend was like banishment to Siberia. Davis Park was at the outer limits of taxi action. People at Davis Park usually stayed put and enjoyed their own forms of frivolity. Rarely did people from other parts of the island go there and even rarer was a fare of more than two people. I suspect there are fares at Davis Park on weekend nights that are still waiting on the beach for the taxi to show up.

Banishment to Davis Park meant being pulled away from the Ocean Beach/Cherry Grove location where the real week end action was happening. Here there was no need to call a taxi. People huddled in groups along the beach front waiting for a taxi, any taxi that might arrive. Pull up to any board-walk that faced the ocean and you could be guaranteed a dozen or more willing passengers ready to go with cash in their pockets. Why waste time and money by going to Davis Park? This attitude didn't endear us to Davis Park customers nor to Everett Wright, and it nearly drove the dispatcher nuts but it avoided significant loss of fares and that was clearly our goal.

Davis Park also presented another scenario for avoidance. Besides being a time drain and money loser, it was the hangout of Everett Wright. Any trip to Davis Park ran the risk of confronting Everett. He had a sixth sense about knowing when one of his cabs was in the vicinity. I think he could identify them by the smell of the gas fumes. A personal inspection was mandatory and obligatory. Everett knew the particulars about every taxi he worked on and insisted on inspecting each cab every chance he got. Every once in a while, I couldn't avoid being caught and could predict the conversation that would ensue

"Why all that salt spray on your windows?" he would say. "You been in the water, right?"

"No," I would reply with an innocent tone in my voice. "It's probably from parking on the beach at night."

"Well stay outta the water." It made no difference how I responded to his questions, when he made up his mind, nothing changed.

He would slowly circle the cab. "How'd you get that dent in the fender?"

"It was there when I picked the cab up this year, Everett, remember?"

"If you put another dent in the cab, I'm gonna have to charge you."

"But Everett" It was wasted time trying to convince him otherwise.

Everett's inspections were meant to intimidate. He didn't have a lot of respect or confidence in college kids. They were all smart-asses with no practical sense. He and Roger were on the same page with this attitude.

Adding to the misery of being at Davis Park was that I got duped into taking one of Everett's fares. They really weren't fares; they were his friends. He had lots of friends. He was loyal to his friends, Mostly they were friends who used to hunt and fish with him and were used to having him do favors.

Everett had his own fare system for his friends. Taxi traffic at Davis Park consisted of hauling luggage or groceries or furniture for Everett's friends from the ferry dock to a boardwalk close by their house. I had to load the stuff as well as unload it. It was a time consuming process, but not one dismissed lightly or with an attitude because these were Everett's friends, and I worked for Everett and surely any disrespect on my part would get back to Everett. Tips were discouraged from Everett's friends. When finished, I turned off my radio, drove as best I could on hidden back sand paths, and avoided returning to any place I suspected Everett might be present. Davis Park was a nightmare.

Drivers studiously avoided other locations as well. Fair Harbor, for instance: somewhat isolated, a nice place for families, and a charming community, but not welcoming for taxis. Fair Harbor had a few quirks that were annoying. It lay toward the far west end of the island, far away from where the action was at the Grove and the Pines. If there was a fare, it meant a long, empty ride down to the community for the pickup. An empty cab earns no cash. Returning a fare to Fair Harbor meant an empty ride back again. Still no cash.

People from Fair Harbor made a point of bad mouthing taxis. They didn't like any vehicles on the beach, as they disturbed their tranquility and isolation. They championed the "Ban cars from the beach" campaign. Taxis, they maintained, were the worst offenders, since they were most visible and active on the beach.

This attitude didn't deter Fair Harbor residents from using our service but it did dictate that one use discretion when reserving a taxi. Fair Harbor callers adhered to certain criteria when contracting for a taxi. (1) The caller would request that the dispatcher schedule the pickup after dark, (2) they requested they meet at the far corner of the community, and (3) they often refused to give a specific name. I attributed these conditions to three causes. (A) They didn't want their neighbors to know they were going down to "sin city" (Cherry Grove), (B) they didn't want to get caught violating the "no vehicles on the beach" campaign, and (C) they were all hypocrites.

Smack in the geographical middle of Fire Island was the community of Point O' Woods. Every trip taken between the communities of Cherry Grove, Fire Island Pines and points west traveled the beach front of Point O' Woods. This meant a lot of traffic, especially on weekends. It was a constant challenge because Point O' Woods was perhaps the oldest community on the Island and its most insular. Point O' Woods was a place frozen in time. It began as an intentional religious/cultural community patterned after the Chateauguay Association whose propose was *"to furnish people with attractions of a summer resort and in addition give them a program of variety and excellence in musical, artistic, scientific, and religious subjects."* The attraction to the residents of Point O' Woods was its idyllic setting and intentional life-style. The homes were all huge, brown-shingled cottages fashioned after those one might expect at Newport, Rhode

Chautauqua!

Island. A six foot high chain link fence, probably constructed to keep residents in rather than intruders out, surrounded the entire complex. According to an article in the New York Times (December 6, 2006) in the 1940's, there was reported to have been a sign that read "No Jews or Dogs Allowed." Neither were Catholics or blacks.

Because the life-style was intentionally insular and family oriented, liquor was not sold inside Point O' Woods, but it was not unheard of for curious residents to occasionally sneak under the fence for an anonymous evening of wild partying next door at Ocean Bay Park. Otherwise, daily life was lived in serene moderation in accordance to strict family values. Residents geared activities around lessons for children--tennis, sailing, swimming, and arts and crafts. And then there was the church. Nearly the entire population attended church, most likely because the tennis courts closed on Sunday morning and sailing lessons postponed. Want to become a member of Point O' Woods Association? You had to be approved by the membership and the first mandate was to have children.

The good people of Point O' Woods made no bones about it – they hated vehicles on their beach. The devised some very creative ways to discourage taxi traffic. They buried boards with protruding nails in the sand tracks hoping for flat tires. During daylight hours, sunbathers would intentionally lie in the tracks forcing drivers to divert around so as not to run over them. Drift-wood piles would suddenly appear as blockades. Such arrogance, as if they personally owned the beach sand. Yet, passing through this area was necessary for the taxi business.

Not to worry. Taxi drivers had vivid imaginations as well. Two could play this game. Imaginative ways were concocted to piss off Point O' Woods dwellers. Most days, the wind blew in off the sea from a southerly direction. Wind noise tended to blot out engine noise and if headed into the wind, the taxi engine was barely audible to the person ahead even from a short distance.

Up ahead, lying peacefully on her stomach sunning her backside was a young lady who just happened to have her swim suit top unsnapped. I slowly approached from the downwind side, and when within only a few feet, I blasted my horn, not once, but many times. Up she jumped in horror to find a contented, sneering, lecherous face staring at her. It was never a pleasant exchange, and I am sure the staid residents of Point O' Woods would have been appalled at her use of the English language.

People in the cab meant profit for a taxi driver. The more people, the more profit. No rules existed for how many people could fit into one taxi at one time. Each driver saw this as a challenge. Who can get the most people in the cab at one time? Sometimes it felt like a sport, each of us vying for the prize for having the largest capacity of passengers at any one time. We often bragged to each other.

"Last night at closing at the Grove," one driver boasted, "I had this fat drunk queer in the back. He was so fat that I laid him out and had seven people sit on top of him."

"I had a group from Ocean beach," another driver stated, "who wanted to go to the Grove. I already had eight people in the cab, but both groups thought it would be real friendly if they all got to ride together. I think I ended up with thirteen happy homos."

"Mr. Bowen from the Pines wanted me to lug his boxes of groceries to his house," Terry told us. "There must have been at least ten boxes. Six other guys said they would pay the fare if they could ride along. They agreed to carry the boxes in their laps just so they wouldn't have to walk home. The back of the jeep dragged sand the whole way."

Each cab had a bench seat in the front. Two people could fit beside the driver. The back seat was designed for three people. That statistic caused little attention. Six could easily squeeze in there when necessary. Behind that seat was a cargo area, a trunk like affair, a cavernous area with a tailgate that opened completely. It was in this area that we became most creative. With proper formations and some body maneuvering, we could load another six to eight people. People had to sit cramped together back there, often with their legs dangling over the tailgate, but what the hell, most customers enjoyed the adventure.

On a busy Saturday night, potential customers waited on the beach as if at a bus stop. I might have a party of six already loaded in the cab, when four more would flag me down as I passed on the beach.

"Oh we thought you were empty," one of them would remark as I stopped to inquire. "We'll wait for the next cab."

"No need for that," I replied. I quickly hopped out of the driver's seat, went to the back of the cab, and lowered the tail gate and made a mental calculation of another twenty dollars.

"But there's no room inside," one of the four protested.

"No problem. Lots of room back here." I gave a hand gesture of welcome to the tail-gate. "These people are going to the same place you are and we all want to get there as soon as possible. Hop In." They were delighted and giggled the remainder of the trip. It was a bonus that they were so willing to comply, probably because they were partially inebriated already.

Sometimes our enthusiasm to fill cabs to overflowing backfired, and things would get a bit testy. It was a Saturday night and calls were coming in like crazy. Paul, the dispatcher, sent out a message telling us there were six people waiting at Beach Plum Walk in Ocean Beach. Paul didn't always know or care which driver answered a call. I headed to the pickup point, and suddenly in front of me were about ten people frantically waving their hands to get my attention. I stopped.

"We want to go to the Grove," they told me.

"Sure," I said. "Hop in." They filled the inside and spilled over to also fill the tailgate.

I was only a few hundred yards away from Beach Plum Walk. The party that called spied my taxi and ran down toward the cab. Before I could get started again, they were on me like a pack of wolves.

"You're the taxi we called, aren't you," they stated. It's wasn't a question as much as a mandate.

"Uh…Yeah, I guess so," I meekly replied, But I'm full and another cab is close behind me. He'll pick you up."

"No, no," one of the alpha males tells me. "We called for

this taxi, and these people just stopped you on the beach, didn't they?"

I tried to weasel out. "I know," I told him in my most apologetic, barely audible voice "But there's another cab right down the beach. See the headlights coming this way?"

"No, that won't do," he insisted. "This is our taxi. Ask the people inside to get out and wait for the next one." This came more as a demand than a request.

From inside the cab, I hear voices. "We ain't moving."

I was about to have a full-fledged revolt on my hands that I was not wanting to referee. Fist fights gave me the willies. I offered more apologies, but to no avail. People were standing their ground. Each side claimed this taxi as their own.

My only recourse was quick action. I jammed the gear into reverse and stepped on the accelerator. The cab lurched backward about twenty yards. I turned the wheel to the right and put the gear in first and plunged forward barely missing the persons standing adjacent to the cab. My window was open and hands full of sand came streaming in, striking the side of my face and landing in my lap. Obscenities followed profusely.

"We have your license number and we're going to report you," I heard as I drove away. The people in back gave them the one finger salute and shouted their own obscenities.

I had nothing to say, but thought to myself that working at McDonalds would be a lot safer. I prayed that I would not be first in line when these same people decided it was time to return home later that evening.

10

Hustling for Fares

The beach was like the wild west in those days. You could do just about anything you liked. The police only came over from the mainland if someone drowned or somebody got killed

---Roger Miskowsky, *Fire Island Tide,* June 22, 2007

No rules exist to regulate taxi drivers on Fire Island. There were a few unwritten expectations however, which came mostly as mandates from Roger and Everett.

"Don't run over sunbathers if you can possibly avoid it."

"Don't drive on the dunes unless you have to drive on the dunes."

"No unsavory hand gestures to anti-beach taxi advocates, unless they give one to you first."

"Never try to cheat the bosses out of money."

Except for the last one, even these simple expectations were mostly ignored. Otherwise, driving a taxi on the beach was free form.

"Make up the rules as you need to," one of the other drivers advised me. "You never know what might happen."

"Like what?" I inquired.

"Like if you meet a nice looking half-drunk chick, and she's not a dyke and she invites you home for a drink or two," he continued. "What are you going to do then? Ain't no rules covering that circumstance, and you better be prepared."

"No, I meant about driving the cab." I tried to sound innocent, but was really attentive to his perspective. It seemed to fit closely into my aspirations for the ideal summer job. I didn't yet know what I would do in a situation like that, but I was hopeful.

White Cap Taxis had no meters in the cabs. No fares where posted inside the taxis nor in the office.

"So how much am I supposed to charge?" I asked the same driver.

"Depends," he said.

"Depends on what?"

"Depends on the distance and the number of people. And it depends on how drunk you think they are."

It didn't come as a complete surprise to me that fares where arbitrarily set since there were no meters and no fare postings. There were some basic expectations. For instance the standard fare from Fire Island Pines to Cherry Grove was a three dollar flat fee or one dollar per person for three or more people. It seemed reasonable then, that fares twice that distance would be twice that amount. Not necessarily so.

"If you have a large group of party people and they seem pretty drunk and in a good mood, you can probably get a lot more. They don't care," the driver told me.

That sounded a bit unethical, and I told him so.

"Sometimes a drunk can't tell the difference between a five dollar bill and a ten. It's not my responsibility to teach him," the driver said. "But if it was the other way around and a ten was expected and he gave me a five, I'd have no hesitation in holding a math class right there. Nothing unethical about that."

Like any business, I learned that taxi fares were market-driven. When demand was greatest, so were the fares. Other times, it took some creative negotiations to reach a fair compromise. Weekday afternoons, for instance, were times when I might be called upon to move some furniture or groceries from the ferry dock to a nearby resident's home.

These were negotiated fares. A price was determined in accordance with criteria I made up myself. The negotiations depended on a variety of factors. I posed questions that went something like this:

"Did I have to load it?"

"How far was the house from the dock?"

"Was the merchandise fragile?"

"Did I have to unload it?"

"How far was the house from the nearest point at which I could park?" (This determined the carrying distance and time.)

"Were they gay or straight?" (Straights liked to carry their stuff and gays didn't.)

In truth, the whole rigmarole was an exercise in stalling. I didn't want the fare and hoped the customer didn't want to hire me. These fares were annoying, took too much time, and were only minimally profitable. People balked at paying more to move their stuff than to move themselves, even when insisting that more care be given their stuff than themselves.

Negotiations began by my writing down (1) how much was to be moved, (2) how far I had to drive, and (3) how valuable the cargo was. I would then feign calculating a fare using some imaginary formula I made up, all the time muttering meaningless numbers under my breath. The whole affair gave an impression of significant reckoning.

"Well sir," I would tell them, "according to my calculations that would come to twenty-two fifty."

"What? That's robbery," the customer would complain.

Then I would propose the selling point. "If you can carry your stuff from the boardwalk to your house, I can cut that if half," I would offer.

"That's a lot more reasonable," would be an expected response.

If the fare was a gay guy, the negotiations took a different slant. Since I knew gays didn't like carrying stuff, unless it was a poodle, I contrived a different strategy. Gay guys wanted me to transport either expensive or fragile stuff, sometimes both – antique furniture, picture frames with beveled glass, small statues of David acquired in a New

York art gallery, or boxes of imported French wine. Breakage was their primary fear. Gays claimed an attachment to their stuff as if it were a family member. The key to profit was the guarantee, convincing them that nothing would get lost, stolen, or broken in transit. So relieved was the guy that his prized possessions arrived unscathed that a very large tip was always expected. The tip so exceeded the fare that quibbling about the fare was unnecessary.

Weekdays were uneventful for taxi drivers. Other than meeting the few ferry boats that arrived each day and transporting families with kids and dogs and beach balls and boxes of food to their rental homes for the week, business was sluggish. Fire Islanders liked to stay put during daylight hours. After a late night of too many gin and tonics, Alexanders, Stingers, Crème de Menthe's, or drinks made with Midori Melon Liqueur, rising before noon was an exception. Once up, residents often greeted the day with a Bloody Mary or two to get the juices flowing and the heart beating. The afternoon was spent on the beach sun-worshipping or browsing the boutiques. Of course, many bars opened early for those who craved conversation about the latest fashions or new Broadway shows.

On Friday nights, a metamorphosis occurred. Fire Island transformed from an idyllic, quiet, laid-back community into one of the East Coast's most notorious party phenomena. For those of us driving taxis, we quickly abandoned all thoughts of protocol and politeness and expediency became our sole motivation. Each driver recognized that profits earned over a weekend greatly exceeded those for the past five days. Competition became intense. Unfortunately, the weekend only drivers arrived, doubling the number of available cabs.

Rivalry was fierce. Friday night boats arrived with hundreds of visitors every hour at Fire Island Pines. The laid back, but party-hardy life- style so notorious for Islanders began as people stepped onto the ferry on the mainland. It was anticipated, no expected, that the weekend partying commenced with the first step on the boat. The ferry ride was a sort of metaphor of anticipation of what was to come. The forty–five minute bay crossing allowed the average gay guy to acquire a high that would probably remained undisturbed until Sunday night when he faced the ubiquitous doldrums of leaving the island and returning to the city. One could earn a considerable summer's profit by just collecting the empty beer bottles on the boat and stashing the recycle deposit. Upon disembarking the ferry, most passengers reveled in their inebriation. Many a Friday night, I watched in amazement and, admittedly, with great glee as departing passengers dropped watches, wallets, groceries boxes, and the occasional poodle into the water.

The more experienced drivers' confronted disembarking gays with an "in your face" approach that I found offensive. I suggested that perhaps we could be more orderly and polite as we waited for fares if we established some taxi protocol like lining our cabs up in orderly fashion and expecting the first customers to disembark to take the first cab in line.

"What kind of bull-shit is that?" one driver remarked. "If you want any fares, you better learn to hustle like the rest of us. Sit in a line? Who you kidding?"

I soon grew tired of other drivers, especially weekend drivers, hustling my fares as I watched in disbelief. As I was leading a willing customer toward my cab, another driver would intercept his suitcases, and march off toward his own cab. Dumbfounded, I stood silent as the other driver led away my prospective customer. I knew I had to become more assertive and deploy my own unique tactics if I were to survive this summer with my self-confidence intact and with some modicum of financial success.

My strategies evolved over time. My confidence improved along with my assertiveness. The key to success was to convince myself that each person exiting the ferry on a Friday night needed a cab; they just hadn't recognized that need. The successful strategy hinged on my conviction that no gay guy enjoys carrying his own stuff, which with both arms already engaged holding Fluffy the poodle and a giant wolfhound tugging at a leash, it was just not possible for him to be responsible for the rest of his stuff. My task and my future success lay in my ability to convince him that even after paying an exorbitant fare, he would be so appreciative of my assistance he would willingly offer up a sizable tip. All I needed now was the gumption to put this stratagem into practice.

I approached the potential fare. "Gee, it looks like you are having trouble carrying all that stuff. Can I give you a hand? My taxi is right over there."

"That would be very nice, darling."

Rule number one: To achieve a maximum tip, always be polite, offer assistance before being asked, and never, never discuss the outrageous taxi fare before you arrive at the destination or after you unload the luggage. Keeping the luggage intact in the cab when discussing the fare served as an insurance policy. I had something he wanted, and he had something I wanted: An even trade.

I envisioned a scenario of the typical gay guy just arriving by ferry after a long week on the job. The theater auditions had not gone as well as expected, and his modeling job collapsed. Add to that the stress of traffic congestion leaving the city, the difficulty finding a legal parking place for the week-end, confronting the anti-gay slogans painted all over the ~~Seville~~ ferry landing, and having to load all his stuff onto the ferry from his car all by himself. Such unimaginable stress. The final straw was watching Fluffy take a shit on the boat and having to clean it up. The humiliation would be overwhelming. He must be exhausted, poor soul. My imagination ran rampant.

"Yes sir, I'm here to help." How appreciative he must feel for my assistance. Appreciative people harbor an obligation to tip well.

Beyond appreciation, another strategy that often worked well I called "act first, ask questions later." I looked for a person nervously eying his belongings that surrounded him on the ferry. I imagined he was thinking, "How will I ever get all this to the house before this weekend is over? If I have to do it myself, I'll be too tired to enjoy the beach and miss all the parties." I approached and courteously engaged him in conversation.

"Can I help you carry these bags off the ferry?"

"Why certainly, hon, just put them on the dock."

I presumed he thought I was either (1) part of the ferry crew just trying to keep passengers happy and safe or (2) a good scout. I didn't announce that I was a taxi driver. I took his bags and quickly placed them in the back of my cab. My strategy was to walk a fine line between assertiveness and helpfulness.

By the time he disembarked from the boat, I had most of his stuff already placed in the cab. When he realized I was a cab driver, his resistance softened. Rather than protest, the response was "What the hell, let's go." Once I had his stuff, I was sure he would follow.

Plans sometimes went dreadfully wrong. If my attempts at being helpful were quickly recognized as hustling by a gay with no intention of hiring a cab, the results were often anything but pretty. I would have the potential fare's luggage in my arms and be disembarking the ferry when he would realize that I was putting his stuff in the back of my cab.

"Thanks, but I don't want a cab," he might say.

I would pretend not to hear him and continue loading his suitcases, boxes of wine, and grocery bags while he wrestled with his large wolfhound.

Then I would hear in an insistent and annoyed tone.

"Hey buddy, what are you, a thief? I told you I didn't want a cab."

"Sorry sir, I thought I was helping."

I would remove his luggage from the cab, place it in the sand next to the dock, and return to the boat in search of another fare. My actions revealed my attitude and did little to endear me to this same person who might request a cab later in the weekend.

Lining up for fares in any semblance of civilized order was an option, but not always an opportunity of which drivers availed themselves. On weekday evenings, calls were so infrequent that drivers usually remained in or near Fire Island Pines, just hanging out, eating take-out from a local restaurant, or just bullshitting while sitting next to each other in our cabs. When a boat arrived, there was a mad scramble to see who could maneuver to the best place for snatching the infrequent fare

Weekend nights, however, rarely did we stay within the confines of one community. Being out on the beachfront allowed us quick access to the best locations quicker. Fares were plentiful then and competition fierce. Despite that people often wanted us to deliver them and their goods at their doorway or as close inside the dunes as possible, on weekend evenings we specifically denied these requests. Our excuses were feeble.

"Would love to be able to do that," we would tell customers, "but regulations don't allow it.

"What regulations?" the customers might ask,

"The police are clamping down on driving over the dunes."

"I saw you driving over the dunes on Tuesday," the same customer might remind us.

"Well, the insurance doesn't allow us to drive anywhere except on the beachfront on weekends because of the many taxis we are running."

"Oh… Okay, the customer would answer, a sense of resignation in his voice.

All of the above had nothing to do with "regulations" and everything to do with expediency; our ability to move about the beach with as much precision and speed as possible, both of which accounted for more fares and greater profit in less time. My livelihood as a taxi driver depended upon how quickly and efficiently I could learn the art of the hustle.

11

Radio Interference

*An African chieftain flew to the United States to visit
the president. When he arrived at the airport, a host of
newsmen and television cameramen met him. One of the
reporters asked the chief if he had a comfortable flight.*

*The chief made a series of weird noises .... "screech,
scratch, honk, buzz, whistle, z-z-z-z-" ... and then added
in perfect English, "Yes, I had a very nice flight."*

*Another reporter asked, "Chief, do you plan to visit
the Washington Monument while you're in the area?"*

*The chief made the same noises ... "screech, scratch,
honk, buzz, whistle, z-z-z-z" ... and then said, "Yes,
and I also plan to visit the White House and the Capitol
Building."*

*"Where did you learn to speak such flawless
English?" asked the next reporter.*

*The chief replied, "Screech, scratch, honk, buzz,
whistle, z-z-z-z ... from the short-wave radio.*

-- Harshita Solanki

There was a line of White Cap Taxis parked on the beach
in front of Cherry Grove. It was about 1:00 A.M. Not much
business at that time of night. It's past the time for bringing

the partygoers down to the Grove and yet not yet time to bring them home again. All the drivers had their radios turned on and tuned into the same frequency. We risked talking with each other so long as we assumed Roger was occupied elsewhere and not listening. "No talking except about business," was his mandate.

"See that chick coming down the stairs?" one of the drivers announced over the radio. All the other drivers turned their heads to look. "She's stunning. What a great body. Think she wants to go for a ride?" he continued.

"Maybe, but not with you," another driver responded. "She's more than a wimp like you can handle."

Another driver piped in. "She's probably a lezzie, Terry. You're closest to being a girl. She's heading for you."

Terry responded. "Smart ass. If she'll do me, don't make any difference if she's AC or DC" (Likes boys and girls).

All the cabs lined up in close proximity, so even without benefit of radios, I could hear all the drivers laughing.

The radios in each cab were not the kind for listening to the news or weather reports or Wolfman Jack and the top twenty hits. These were the short-wave variety. I had no concept of what "short wave" meant or how they differed from "long wave"; or any other kind of wave designation. Such understandings were way beyond my pay scale. I couldn't explain how voices transmitted over any kind of radio. It remained for me a marvelous mystery of technology.

Our radios shared a common origin with walkie talkies, just one degree better than the two tin cans connected by a string that I pretended to use to communicate with my brother as a kid. When they functioned properly, they allowed the base operator to talk with all the cabs at once. There could be no private conversations between two drivers; whatever one person said was heard by all others, depending, of course, that they had their radios on. There were those times, more frequently than I anticipated, that I left my radio on with the microphone dangling near my seat and accidentally, or at least unintentionally, sat on it. My rear end depressed the on button of the microphone rendering every voice, burp, or other bodily function easily audible throughout the entire system.

Despite being necessary for the taxi business, these radios occasionally caused considerable frustrations. Radio interference, for instance, was the source of much miscommunication and vexation. Depending upon the weather, conversations could become garbled, cut short, or non-existent. It wasn't so much from our own system, but rather the interference from other companies using short wave radio frequencies similar to our own. Each entity or base station was assigned a different frequency, but the distance between frequencies was very narrow. Channel 12, for instance, might be only a hairs breath away from channel 14, so close that often the two channels functioned as one. I never understood the finer points of the physics of the situation, but these frequencies intermingled with our own.

Good weather produced the greatest interference. That sounds incongruent, but here's my personal explanation. On a nice clear day, excessive chatter from competing frequencies was prolific. My theory was that radio waves, like ocean waves, met with resistance. Like ocean waves bumping against the shoreline, radio waves met resistance when transmitted through the atmosphere. They bumped against heavy air or fog or mist. On crystal clear days there was little to stop them. On foggy days or when the humidity was high or during rainstorms, the waves had a much more difficult time pushing through the dense air. The result was that interference from competing frequencies was minimal during days when clouds were abundant and greater when skies remained clear. I had no scientific proof of this theory, but it sure sounded reasonable to me.

Radio interference was often more than annoying; sometimes it was downright frightening. If I was sitting in my cab on the beachfront, it only made sense to have the radio turned on in case a call for a fare came through. I needed to be prepared and ready to roll at a moment's notice. On weekdays, the radio, despite being on, remained fairly quiet. Few calls came through. One moment I would be sitting peacefully in my cab, perhaps reading a book, or listening to the sounds of the crashing waves while thinking about getting laid that evening. And then, with no warning, great squawking sounds blared from the radio so suddenly and with such volume that it startled me. I would leap up in my seat and hit my head on the roof of the cab or bang my knees on the steering wheel. That hurt. I never thought a radio could be so dangerous.

Other times the radios presented opportunities for creativity. As I sat in my cab on a sunny afternoon with nary a cloud in the sky, I would hear, "Joey, where's the ladders?" or "I'm headed for the job in Astoria," or "Can't meet with them until after 3:00." None of it made any sense. It was radio interference from some plumbing company or an electric distributor business over on the mainland that had short wave radios with frequencies very close to our own. And it always occurred on crystal clear days. It often came as a complete surprise and quite disquieting. But it stimulated my imagination. I wanted to respond.

The Federal Communications Commission was supposed to monitor these frequencies and make adjustments if too many remained in such close proximity that they interfered with each other, but they didn't always get it right. The technology wasn't yet perfected adequately.

When interference did occur, it was like listening to one end of a phone conversation. The base radio of the competing company or business was powerful enough for me to pick up, but the mobile unit in the individual truck was not. Listening to half a conversation was plain frustrating. One such conversation might be like this:

"We need sixteen feet of half inch pipe." These were words I might intercept from a plumbing supply company's base radio. Silence followed during which I assumed the mobile unit was responding.

After the silence, the base might say, "Then make it three quarter."

Again silence.

Once again the base would reply, "It's the upstairs bathroom."

Silence.

"Then Henry will have to clean it out, "came from the base unit.

More silence. It annoyed me to no end to continually hear half a conversation. So I made up my own dialogue to fill in the silences.

Radio man: "We need sixteen pieces of half inch pipe."

My imagination: "Shit won't fit through half inch pipe."

Radio man: "Then make it three quarters."

My imagination: "Which toilet is overflowing?"

Radio man: "It's the upstairs bathroom."

My imagination: I ain't putting my hands down there."

Radio man: "Then Henry will have to clean it out."

Having access to radios proved to be somewhat enigmatic and, depending upon how we used them, not always the convenience they were intended. Radio waves are public conveyances. So long as one had access to a short wave radio receiver, there were few regulations on their use and fewer rules regarding the protocol of what could or could not be discussed, with the exception of Roger's mandates. No swearing which we did not always adhere. No private conversations. The radio was intended as a tool of business, but the rule was universally dismissed whenever one had a good joke to share.

Each individual cab radio had a talk button which allowed a driver to speak and be heard by all other drivers. With the talk button released, the radio was a receiver only. When a driver received a conversation, protocols required that one repeat the phrase "10-4" ("I got it") and then release the talk button. The rule was one person talked at a time.

We had great difficulty abiding by this simple rule. Not that we were incapable of understanding the necessity and usefulness of it, but rather because we exhibited no tolerance when it came to seeking a customer. Let's say there might be six of us drivers cruising the beach or sitting at the dock on a Thursday night looking for fares. It's a particularly slow evening and no one is making much money. Suddenly, Paul, the dispatcher, announces a potential fare which broadcast to all the radios at the same time. Every driver pushed his on button at the same time

"Party of six needs to be picked up at Sunset Walk in Ocean Beach," Paul says. "Who's got it?"

Instantly, quicker than an epiphany, six drivers press their talk buttons at the same time. Six simultaneous "I got its" sound to Paul in the office as a jumble of mumbling sounds emanating from a hyena in heat. He understands nothing. There is a moment of silence as each driver waits to hear a confirmation from Paul that he has the fare.

Instead Paul says, "I can't hear you. You're all talking at once. Who's got it?"

Again, in perfect sync comes a cacophony of replies, "I got it." Again they are unintelligible to Paul.

This time Paul sounded annoyed. "You can't all talk at once. Nothing comes through but crap I can't understand. Now one of you tell me you will take this call. Who's got it?"

Nothing changes. No matter how often this occurs or how insistent Paul becomes, each driver continued to push the talk button at the same time. In an attempt to be heard above the others, each driver begins to yell into the mike, as one often does when speaking with a person who doesn't understand English. It took all of Paul's patience to filter through the jumble of voices and eventually assign the fare to one of the drivers. Even then, protestations flew out by vitriolic drivers who felt slighted. Of course no one listened because each driver cursed and complained at the same time.

Sometimes Paul, feeling spiteful himself over being ignored, wouldn't assign the fare to any driver. Soon, all six drivers appeared at the same location almost simultaneously. Paul's attitude: "let them figure it out."

Six drivers at the same location for the same fare presented a dilemma of great proportions. Who arrived at the location first was of little consequence. Politeness was never a necessary attribute for becoming a driver.

"Paul said the fare was mine," I might say. I had no reluctance about embellishing or downright lying. "If you don't believe me, ask him." That was more of a tentative threat than a statement of intent.

"I was here first," one of the other drivers might interject.

"Childish bullshit," still another might put forward.

Finally the ultimate coup de grace. "You guys keep arguing," one of the drivers interjected. "I got the fare in my cab. See you. "

No one actually knew who Paul assigned the fare to, and I suspected that Paul was not about to say. The radio clutter made sure of that.

12

Encounters, Conflicts, and Other Distractions

*Roads between the communities had never been
developed on Fire Island, but until the mid-Sixties jeeps
were allowed to operate up and down the beach between
them as a taxi service. They were almost like amusement
park rides as they went at what seemed like breakneck
speed and were barely under control as they swerved and
slid through loose sand. During the day they drove close
to the edge of the water and exercised some care, however
at night they drove higher up on the beach and with
a great deal less care. Walking on the beach at night,
we had kept a sharp eye on them as they approached as
pedestrians were difficult to see in the pitch dark until
a taxi was almost upon you. There were often near
accidents, and in July 1966 the famous (gay) poet Frank
O'Hara-an early contributor the Evergreen Review was
hit by a beach taxi at night and killed.*

--*What a Wonderful Town, PT. II.* Adapted from the work
of Joseph A. Fields and Jerome Chodorov.

No denying it, taxis on Fire Island were immune to most
traffic regulations. They did drive mainly at night because
that's when the public wanted to go places. It was the tides,

not the time of day that dictated whether to drive up near the dunes of down by the water's edge. Low tide afforded a hard surface close to the water which permitted jeeps to travel faster. More speed meant the possibility of more customers during any designated time frame. We did not intentionall*y* condone reckless driving but neither was it condemned. That a taxi killed Frank O'Hara is open to dispute. No records indicate that the "beach buggy" that slammed into him was a taxi. Hence, the above quote may be biased conjecture

Despite the competition, there exists camaraderie between cab drivers, just as there does between competing sports players, stockbrokers, auto salespeople, or ministers. Each feels some connectedness with the others through mutual circumstances. If cab drivers held an annual convention or trade show, I feel certain they would enjoy swapping stories, sharing tricks of the trade, confessing to mutual problem areas, and embellishing stories about celebrities and eccentrics they have met. They can be just as consumed with work-related experiences as any other profession

Taxi drivers in most cities, I have observed, are a congenial lot. When parked in a line at the airport or in front of some downtown hotel, I have never failed to see drivers conversing with each other. In my imagination, I hear them relating tales of the many strange requests they must get, swapping information about shortcuts to new neighborhoods, or laughing aloud about the tailpipe that just fell off the cab in front of them. Certainly there must be competition among them, but it doesn't deter from the camaraderie.

On Fire Island, establishing a fraternity among cab drivers was a lot more difficult. Most times it didn't exist. In our conversations, when trying to be civilized and polite, we exchanged verbally that certain expectations should to be adhered to an orderly line at the ferry terminals, taking turns answering radio calls, or not hustling another driver's customers – but seldom, if at all, did we abide by these expectations. It was interesting conversation but without consequences. Pissing off other drivers was not meant intentionally; it just happened.

I held a particular animosity toward the weekend drivers. These guys held full-time week day jobs on the mainland--plumbers, carpenters, auto mechanics--and to earn extra cash, or maybe to get a break from their kids and wives, they came to the island on Friday nights. They proclaimed they needed beer money. It was obvious to me their real intention was to loiter in the hopes of scoring with some of the ladies without their wives' knowing.

My rancor toward weekend drivers stemmed from feeling that they were interlopers and intruders. They were not necessary. It felt unfair that I should have to put in fifteen-hour days during the week with a lot of unpaid hours of waiting time, and always be accessible to clients when they needed a cab to the meat rack at 2:00 A.M. and then have to share the lucrative weekends with part-timers. Besides that, they were usually older men who had worked as drivers for a few years and such status enabled them to claim the better jeeps.

Jerry was a weekend driver, a local guy about my own age who worked construction Monday through Friday. Jerry had two strikes against him of particular note. First, he was very good looking, and he attended Princeton University. Secondly, he was very bright and articulate, built like an accomplished body builder, and had a gorgeous smile that framed his perfect white teeth. As a driver in a predominately gay community, these were attributes that garnered great attention and with which I could not compete. He was out of my league, and the gay guys loved him. God how I hated him.

Jerry had a very assertive personality and simply oozed confidence. I rationalized that his approachability with gay guys was a façade, that in fact he abhorred them. He used language that was as homophobic as any I had ever heard, but never in the presence of a gay guy. He knew how to manipulate them, however, and they ogled over him like a boy with a new puppy. For me, who still harbored a streak of awkwardness with strangers and gay men, watching Jerry work his charms on gay guys was like observing a consummate magician performing his magic on an unsuspecting audience. My blood ran green with envy.

Jerry and I had our encounters. I was returning to Fire Island Pines with a fare from Cherry Grove. The tide was high so riding on the hard sand down by the surf was not possible. Instead, I clung to the tire ruts the jeeps made up close to the dunes. The ruts were like train tracks and driving in them was less of a strain on the engine than driving ambiguously through the soft sand. In my rear view mirror, I noticed a White Cap taxi approaching quickly from behind. One of the expectations I had grown used to was that taxis followed, but did not pass each other, while driving in the same direction in the same tracks. Like sheep, jeeps followed the one in front all the way to the ferry landing in Fire Island Pines. I was on track to be the first one returning. I expected the cab behind to follow me.

I noticed the cab closing fast on my tail. It was now almost touching my bumper. I could see Jerry with his toothy grin in my rear view mirror. I figured he would slow down, but just as he was about to ram my rear bumper, he turned his cab sharply to the left, jumped the tracks, and started passing me. Usually when outside the tracks, the jeep engine labors in the soft sand and slows down.

But Jerry didn't slow down. How was that possible, I wondered? Despite giving my jeep extra throttle, Jerry managed to pass by, flashing a grin as he did. His assertive maneuver and clear disregard for driving expectations really pissed me off. One more episode of weekend drivers displaying flagrant aggressiveness I found annoying, frustrating, and intolerable.

Arriving at the Pines, I found Jerry already in line at the ferry landing. One's position in line usually determined when you could count on the next fare. The further up the line, the quicker you got the next customer. I noticed a slight opening between Jerry's cab and the one in front of him. I attempted to nose my cab into that space, claiming a position in line I thought was rightfully mine.

"No cutting," came a chorus of shouts from the other drivers.

"I'm not cutting. Jerry passed me on the way in."

"Yeah right, sure thing." A chorus of insults came from the rest of the drivers. "Get to the rear," they told me in no uncertain terms.

I moved my jeep to the back of the line. I felt like a kindergarten student admonished for taking a toy from the sandbox that wasn't mine. The affair was as embarrassing as it was annoying. I could see Jerry grinning. I vowed not to let this happen again.

Not long afterwards, another circumstance arose. The next weekend, Jerry again was a weekend driver. It happened that while traveling in the same set of tracks, but going in opposite directions, Jerry and I came face to face. As our cabs bore down on each other, it quickly became apparent Jerry was not going to give way and let me pass in the tracks. My stubbornness prevailed. I would not give way either. Not this time. I needed revenge. I was determined not to balk.

We each came to an abrupt halt with our front bumpers kissing each other. We both had fares in our cabs. For one of us to move aside, I knew would benefit both of us financially as we could then deliver our fares and be ready for new customers. It was a weekend evening, and timeliness was essential. We each stood to lose money by standing still.

We were at an impasse. We sat still glaring at each other. Jerry then stuck his head out the window and yelled toward me, "Get that piece of shit ought of the way."

"Screw you," I yelled back. "You move."

There was no protocol that addressed this confrontation, other than what occurred spontaneously. Neither of us seemed poised to act courteously. My emotions ran high. I was angry. Even if I had a pregnant mother in the cab who just broke her water and needed to be rushed to a hospital, I was not about to budge. My distain for weekend drivers and especially Jerry ignited my frenzy and I lost all sense of composure and rationality.

We sat glowering at each other.

"Can we just get going? I heard my passenger say from the back seat of my cab. He spoke rather meekly, yet with the determination of one who was losing patience. I began to realize how much of an ass I was making of myself in front of a paying customer. He must have sensed the animosity between Jerry and me and was fearful that we might come to blows.

I took a deep breath and exhaled slowly. Reason was returning to my composure. I shifted into reverse, backed the jeep up a few yards, and proceeded to drive around Jerry's cab. Jerry remained stationary. As I passed him I heard his nasty laugh obviously directed at me and then the word "sucker." I was fuming. I lost again.

Eventually I made my peace with Jerry. My animosity toward him morphed into a restrained admiration, though still with a bit of suspicion. I was strangely fascinated by him, an almost mystical allure. I began to model my own behavior after what I thought were his strengths. I tried going shirtless with the hope that my upper body might resemble his, I became more flirtatious toward gay men, and I emulated his swagger in my walk and talk. Such behavior, however, only resulted in my being further ignored by the very people I wanted to impress. Gay men took no notice of me. It felt like I was an imposter.

One has to be careful what one wishes for sometimes. A few years after our driving careers ended with White Cap Taxi, Jerry was arrested and convicted of killing his wife and two daughters. Had I any notion that such behavior could be exhibited by him, I never would have allowed him to stay overnight at our house at Water Island.

What camaraderie that existed between drivers sometimes took a rather bizarre turn. Those I had pegged as my greatest competition proved to be trusted allies. The first year I drove for White Cap Taxi, we faced some stiff rivalry from an upstart company called Green Top Taxi (real creative branding). There was little imagination in the naming of the taxi businesses. Fortunately, only two Green Top cabs were functional along with two drivers, Ralph, the owner, and Sonny. Sonny was the driving force behind the competition. He was a unique character. That he always looked scruffy, unwashed, and almost mangy was an understatement. His body odor announced his presence ahead of time. He smelled like a cross between a cat's litter box and the day after in a beer hall.

Maturity was not Sonny's strong suit. He made it clear to all by his attitudes and actions that Peter Pan was his idol and he never wanted to grow up. Sonny never told his age, but I guessed him to be in his mid-thirties. He epitomized the ultimate beach bum. He claimed to live in a squatter's shack he built himself from driftwood he collected along the beachfront. It was situated on land near Skunk Hallow, land that he didn't own but claimed as his because he had lived on it the required number of years. Squatter's rights, under certain conditions, still had some legal authority in those days.

Sonny's life exhibited no focus other than existing for the moment. Yesterday was gone, forget it. Tomorrow doesn't yet exist. Today was sufficient. That was Sonny's credo. Any money he made driving the cab, he spent spontaneously on items that he fancied at the moment - a barbecue grill that he gave away two weeks later, a surfboard that he used one time and then burned for firewood at a beach party, an expensive pair of sunglasses that he dropped in the water and made no effort to retrieve - so that by the end of the summer he had no savings to be used for the lean winter months.

Sonny's sexuality was a matter of conjecture. His appearance and demeanor was that of a thug, but his relationship with gay men gave a different impression. We assumed, considering his flair for the dramatic, that he was probably AC/DC. Sexually, he could go either way. He liked to hang around young boys but was not immune to flirtations with pretty girls as well.

Without an air of ambivalence, he constantly taunted gay men. He openly and flagrantly insulted, ridiculed, and heckled just about every gay man or lesbian with which he came in contact, yet, none of them appeared to take offense. It was as if they recognized that he was one of them, which gave him license to be obnoxious without prejudice.

Of Friday night's, taxis were lined up near the Fire Island Pines ferry dock awaiting the weekenders to arrive and unload. Sonny somehow always managed to maneuver his Green Top Taxi near the front of the line. As the ferries approached the landing, Sonny would yell at the top of his voice to those on the approaching boat "Here come the fairies, and I don't mean the boats." Calls resonated from those on board the boat: "Sonny, your ass is grass, sweetie," or "We fairies are just waiting to get a piece of you." Back and forth would go the banter, with Sonny always seeking to be as humiliating as possible. The gay men never seemed to take offense at Sonny's insinuations. None of the rest of the drivers dared comment in such brazen style. Since we weren't gay, gay-bashing was offensive.

The Green Top Taxi Company did not survive a second summer, and Sonny ended up driving for White Cap. He took some getting used to, but most of the drivers adjusted to him, despite his arrogance and lack of personal grooming. Conflicts were minimal. He never ceased his abusive language and intimidation both to and about gay people and eventually became a legend or at least tolerated and marginally enjoyed by the gay community. His sexuality never was determined absolutely. But it seemed of little consequence, considering that the gay community, the life-blood of the taxi business, paid it no attention.

When he switched allegiance and became a driver for White Cap, we managed to form an alliance. Just as Sonny used to wrangle fares away from us by his blatant offensiveness, he now used the same tactic as a means to secure fares for the rest of the drivers who worked for White Cap. Those seeking similar goals often end up as strange bedfellows.

13

Fishing on Fire Island

Reasons: WHY FISHING IS BETTER THAN SEX.

No matter how much whiskey you've had, you
*   can still fish.*
The Ten Commandments don't say anything
*   against fishing.*
Nobody expects you to fish with the same partner
*   for the rest of your life.*
There are no fishing-transmitted diseases.
Nobody will ever tell you that you will go blind
*   if you fish by yourself.*

--Jim "Lead Rod" Boland, Sr.

My father was an avid fisherman. I never knew if fishing
for him was a sport or a diversion. Pop was not good at
relaxing when on vacation; he always had a project to
complete. Projects took priority over hanging out with the
family. I suspected that family time was more of a chore then
painting the outside of the house. When relaxation, other
than work, did occur to him, fishing became his time away
from family and other preoccupations. It was his time to be
alone with his own thoughts. He always liked fishing alone,

usually early in the morning or just before sunset. We had abundant fishing poles, but he never invited anyone to go with him.

I don't know if I inherited Pop's love of fishing or it was the intrigue of being alone, but fishing became my chosen diversion as well. If I inherited any part of the fishing experience from my father, it was the experience of being alone. My interest heightened when I won a fishing outfit as a result of having the lucky number on a raffle ticket I bought the first summer I drove for White Cap. The Davis Park Casino held a barbecue outing for residents each July 4th and sold raffle tickets for prizes. My prize was a new surfcasting pole, a reel, and some tackle appropriate for ocean fishing.

Rarely did anyone have much luck fishing along the beachfront. Fishing in the surf meant wading waist-deep out into the waves, heaving your lure as far as possible beyond the breakers, and then reeling the line in again. One repeated this process over and over until one's arms felt likely to fall off. I never knew for sure, but local lore dictated that high tide was the best time for fishing. Most times, my father fished according to the time of day rather than the time of the tides. Neither time afforded him much luck. That's when I knew he wasn't serious about fishing but down right serious about his time alone.

I followed a similar pattern. Having my own new fishing outfit became my excuse for leaving parents behind after supper on my days off from driving the taxi and spending time alone wading in the warm waters, just thinking and casting, mostly thinking. I remember one time many years previous when my friend Johnny caught a hammerhead shark in the surf just off Water Island. He wasn't fishing for sharks. No one does that purposefully. It just happened. The excitement it generated drew people from all over the community, along with their Brownie Hawkeye cameras.

According to local lore fishing in the surf was best done under particular circumstances. What determined the ideal conditions were three factors: (1) A flock of birds circling and diving into the sea, an indication that bait fish were near the surface; (2) Bait fish near the surface indicated larger fish were chasing them into towards the shore and the bait fish swam near the surface in an attempt to escape being eaten by the larger ones below. (3) The swirling of the ocean water caused by the foregoing circumstances. The turmoil of the ocean water and the birds diving into the water was a tell-tale sign that large fish were present and it was time to go fishing. This sounded like complex factors totally unintelligible by the average Joe, but it was really quite simple when observed from a passing jeep.

I kept my newly acquired fishing pole and reel neatly stuffed under the back seat of the taxi just in case – just in case the above circumstances ever presented themselves in the proper order, and the moon and stars lined up in a position that indicated that it was time to go fishing. I wanted to be prepared. That's the thing about fishing: one never knows when contemplating fishing can become actually catching some fish.

I had just finished dinner at home and was returning to the Pines to resume a usual slow weekday evening, transporting people back and forth from the Pines to Cherry Grove. I was about a mile past Water Island, cruising slowly in the soft sand ruts up near the dunes. The tide was coming in, prohibiting driving close to the breaking waves. A few hundred yards ahead, I could see a flock of birds circling in a large cluster just beyond the breaking surf. It was worth investigating.

As I got closer, I drove down by the surf's edge without getting my wheels in the water. I could see swirling water with birds circling above. Soon the birds began diving into the water as if attacking small fish near the surface. The water below the birds began churning with activity. I knew immediately these were the omens of active fish disturbance making the circumstances just right, and big fish had to be present.

I brought my taxi to a halt about one hundred feet east of where the birds were circling. Intuition told me the whole mass of swirling water and hungry fish was moving slightly toward the east and inward toward shore. I retrieved my rod and reel, assembled them, and attached a lure to the end of the line. I removed my boat shoes without rolling up my pants. I waded into the rolling surf waist-deep. With a giant heave, I cast the lure as far out into the swirling water as possible. Immediately I began to reel in the lure. After a few cranks of the reel handle, I felt a definite pull on the rod. It bent almost in half. I knew I had a good size fish or I had picked up some very heavy flotsam from the bottom. I continued reeling while walking backwards toward more shallow water.

I reeled in about half of the line when suddenly the leaping of a fish surprised me. It completely left the water, flopped back down, and then leaped out again. I caught a glimpse of the greenish blue of his back and the silver on his sides and knew immediately it was a Bluefish. I thought him to be at least two feet long, if not larger. He continually surged from the waves into the air and then back into the water. "Holy shit," was all I could muster to say. I continued reeling in and walking back toward shore at the same time, hoping I could land the fish before he broke my line or somehow got unhooked. My arms were aching. The pull was so great I could hardly turn the crank on the reel.

I stopped cranking and held the line taut while I continued walking backward until I pulled the fish completely out of the water. Perhaps not the full two feet I imagined, but a good eighteen inches long. It took all my energy to disentangle the hook from the fish's mouth as he flopped incessantly in the sand. Holding the slippery fish seemed impossible until I filled my hands with sand which made holding him manageable. Eventually I released the lure from his mouth. I heaved the fish up on the dry sand where he remained flopping, but safely away from the water

I waded back into the waves and cast the lure again as close to the middle of the swirl of water as possible. I could see birds dropping like stones toward the water, pausing for a split second, and then ascending with a small fish in their beaks. I could see fish tails slapping the surface right where the birds were landing on the water. Clearly this was an indication of a school of large fish feasting on the smaller bait fish.

Bluefish were the dominant variety in the surf off Fire Island. These fish were noted for their "schooling," traveling in large bunches. Bluefish often feed on large schools of baitfish, creating a disturbance known as blitzing in the water. In an attempt to escape, small fish leap into the air while the bluefish churn up the water with tails and snapping jaws. During these feeding frenzies, the water actually looks like it is boiling. When these fish ate, they did so ravishingly. They caused a commotion in the water so disturbing it looked like a whirlpool was forming on the surface. I had been told that they can appear at any time during the summer months, feed for thirty to forty five minutes, and then disappear.

This was not my first encounter with Bluefish. For fun and excitement, I used to string an old fishing pole my father allowed me to have with the basic equipment—line, hook, pole, bobber, and bait--and fish off the end of the dock in the bay. The fish we caught we called snappers. Only later did I learn that snappers where actually baby Bluefish.

My window of opportunity was limited. The whole mass was slowly moving toward the east. I knew I had but a few minutes to catch these fish; otherwise, they would be long gone. With my next cast, I immediately began to retrieve the lure as soon as it hit the water. I snagged another fish and began reeling it in. As the fish approached the shallow water near the breaking waves, I could see that I had hooked it sideways. The fish didn't bite the bait I threw but rather because the school was so thick with fish, my lure caught the fish in the side of the belly as I was reeling in the line. It made no difference to me.

For the next fifteen minutes, I continually cast into the swirl of feasting Blue fish and with each cast caught another fish, sometimes in the mouth, but just as frequently in the stomach or by the tail. At the end of fifteen minutes, I had accumulated a dozen large Blue fish, which still flopped helplessly on the sand where I threw them away from the water's edge.

Just as quickly as they came, they disappeared. Almost instantly, the water calmed and the birds flew away. No matter how many additional casts I made – nothing.

I packed up my new rod and reel and stashed it in the back of the jeep. Twelve large Bluefish lay groveling in the sand, some half dead and others fully spent. I recognized I needed to get them cleaned and under refrigeration very soon, or the warm air would bake them right on the beach. Fortunately I still had last Sunday's *New York Times* in the taxi. I unfurled some of the paper and laid it across the tailgate. I placed all the fish on the newspaper. Why I was so concerned about keeping the taxi free of fish guts and smell, I don't know. Cleanliness was not one of my priorities.

I returned home with the fish. Mom and Pop were impressed, even more so than I was excited.

"We can give a couple to the neighbors, and a few to Uncle Harvey, and maybe one or two to the Donovans," Mom said. "Soon as you get them cleaned, let me know and I'll tell them."

Catching fish was a diversion I could definitely appreciate. Cleaning fish was a different story.

14

Days Off and Nights Out

To go out with the setting sun on an empty beach
is to truly embrace your solitude.

--Jeanne Moreau

Sleep deprivation was a major concern for me. It wasn't that I always felt tired. I didn't, but just the realization that I was existing on only five or six hours of sleep each night caused me much anxiety. Part of it was psychological, I am sure, and recognizing I was surviving on less than ten hours of sleep had an effect on my thinking. Just the thought made me apprehensive. I was a college student and college students, with the exception of final exam weeks, should sleep a minimum of eight to ten hours every day for maximum effective behavior. I was an accomplished sleeper after many years of practice. Napping in the afternoon was a possibility, but the nature of the job was that pay depended on working, and working meant being ready at any moment for a fare. So napping on the job had its drawbacks.

I insisted on one day off each week. Neither Roger nor Everett was pleased with this request, so it took some convincing. Roger proved to be the most skeptical.

"What do you mean, you want a day off. I don't get no day off," Roger barked back at me when I broached the possibility of having one day off. I was hesitant to ask but was intent on being able to savor at least a little of the party time available. As a taxi driver, I spent six days each week noting when and where people went when seeking a good time, the places they congregated when reconciling their longing for merriment. To me, it felt like a shame and waste if I never got a chance to at least attempt to indulge myself. How could I justify a summer spent at the beach if I had no embellished stories to relate of wild merrymaking.

"I know I'll lose some money but if I take Tuesdays off, there is hardly any business those nights anyway," I responded to Roger.

"You mean you want the other drivers, like Terry to have to work for you?"

"I'm sure that will be just fine with them," I said. "They get to make more money that day because I won't be there to compete with them,"

"You college kids, all you think about are having a good time. You don't know what real work is like. When I was your age, I worked seven days a week just to help out my parents. Never asked for a day off. They wouldn't let me even if I did ask." Roger had a way of making you feel like a slouch when you wanted something, even when you had a good story to go with the request.

I chose Tuesday because it turned out, on average, to be the slowest day of the week, and my minimally functioning brain, due to lack of sleep and the need for a strong dose of healthy play time, did some logical calculations concluding I would lose the least amount of money on this day. This thought reverberated well with me, but I needed to convince Roger to accept the circumstances without making me feel guilty. My ploy was to show him that I needed that one day if I were to give him my best the other six days. I did some whining about how I got so tired and felt sick when I worked seven days and wasn't able to give the job my best effort. When presented with a logical argument, Roger usually balked as a matter of principle, but when confronted with a pathetic plea for showing mercy, he was more than accommodating. So I took Tuesdays off.

My first mission on Tuesdays was to sleep as long as possible, which wasn't always easy. My father and mother considered sleeping late to be a broken biblical Commandment comparable to coveting, adultery or worse yet, not honoring thy Father and Mother. Sleeping past seven thirty was a sure sign of moral degeneration, a potential venial sin (that's one committed with intent) for which my parents blamed themselves for being inadequate disciplinarians. I remember while growing up my mother admonished me many times when I failed to wake up and actually get out of bed at the same time that the sun rose. My parents dropped subtle hints that I must be heading toward some kind of waning in body and mind because only alcoholics, drug users, and other derelicts of various persuasions failed to get up early in the morning.

"Sleeping all the time atrophies your mind," my father would tell me. I think he found that word in a magazine and liked the sound if it.

"You can't get done what you have to do before lunch," my mother rebuked me, "if you don't get up before noon. People who sleep late don't do well in school. I know that for a fact." She was convinced that late sleepers turned into bums because they were awake only half their lives. Mom couldn't stand the idea that anyone, much less her own son, would think about sleeping until afternoon. It must be debased and symptomatic of some approaching mental illness.

On Tuesdays, my parent's urge to wake me early was out of control. There would be clanging of pots and pans in the downstairs kitchen under the ruse that Mom was cooking. Mom hated to cook; she only did so reluctantly or out of guilt. The clanging was her reflexive manner to show her disapproval of my late sleeping. Other times there would be the sound of a hammer driving nails into the side of the house. I am sure that Pop intentionally chose eight a.m. to repair the shingles just so the noise would so annoy me that I would get out of bed. The shingles had been broken for years and yet he showed no inclination to fix them except on Tuesday mornings. Their attempts to awaken me were overt but never acknowledged, clear examples of passive-aggression. Eventually, and only with great sighs of reluctance, a lot of moaning and groaning, a few choice unrepeatable phrases, and some slamming of the furniture, I rose from the bed, got dressed in my bathing suit, and went downstairs.

Since it felt like morning to me, I wanted to eat breakfast. This disturbed Mom even more. "It's one in the afternoon. Your father has already eaten his lunch, and you want breakfast?" Despite her protestations, her guilt always won out. It was her task in life to care for her children, despite what bums they might have become. She equated food with love. Two eggs, toast and coffee were on the table in moments. Breakfast was very important to me. I figured that I had much I wanted to do after breakfast, and despite what time of day it might be, I couldn't do what needed doing after breakfast until after breakfast. So breakfast was a priority to begin the day.

After breakfast, I needed a nap. That's what mattered on days off. Our house had a wonderful glassed-in front porch with two sleeper sofas and oodles of pillows scattered about them. When opened, the ocean breeze easily blew through the large windows. It was always cool on that side of the house. Naps were much better when you fell asleep on top of the bedding, especially when you are trying to read, and just can't keep your eyes open. You fell asleep with the book lying open on your chest. Nothing was more restful or comforting for me than an afternoon nap with an open book resting on my chest, along with a preponderance of snoring without interruptions by other people annoyed with my noise.

Despite that my Mom loathed cooking, she habitually prepared diner exactly at six o'clock. This met with my father's schedule because he liked to have his cocktail hour exactly at five-thirty and expected dinner to be ready immediately following. Cocktail hour lasted precisely thirty minutes, no shorter and no longer. Pop was a slave to routine. It always began with clams on the half shell, dug up that very afternoon from the bay, shucked just before being eaten, and covered with a spicy cocktail sauce and horseradish. The feel of a mushy, live clam sliding down my throat without having to even chew sent quivers up my spine. I loved every morsel. Accompanying the clams were whisky sours, usually at least two which immediately affected Mom and caused her to be more than a little tipsy. Despite her inebriation, dinner was on the table at six o'clock sharp.

This met with my schedule as well. I couldn't do what had to be done after dinner until after dinner. I reserved early Tuesday evenings for fishing. I had my new surf pole which I had won at a raffle at the Davis Park Casino earlier that summer. I think it was to raise money for equipment for the volunteer fire department. Or maybe it was to reimburse the casino for the many broken glasses and bay windows that happened each summer by the more rowdy patrons. I don't remember the exact circumstances for the raffle, but I cherished that rod and reel as the only thing I had ever won.

There was something inexplicably good about the feeling of being in the surf up to my waist, casting out beyond the incoming waves as the sun set over the dunes. With the exception of the one day of Bluefish mania, rarely did I ever get a strike, so it couldn't have been the thrill of catching fish that motivated me. I think it was the isolation. Nobody else was on the beach at that time. I was alone with the breaking waves and could gaze solemnly at the far expanse of ocean over the horizon. I remember the feeling of connection. With my feet standing in the water at the edge of this shore, I felt linked with all the other shores this same water touched-- England, Africa, and Spain. It felt like a living dichotomy, isolated and connected at the same time. Besides the philosophical high, surf-casting was the only exercise I got, unless you count shifting gears on the taxi. Fishing served as a transition between daytime and nighttime. Fishing at the end of the day ushered in the beginning of my night life.

Growing up on Fire Island, I never lacked for things to do. Playing on the beach, swimming, kite flying, fishing for snappers off the dock, tying strings to horseshoe crab's tails to pull toy boats through the water, building sand forts in the dunes where my friends and I could throw Coke bottles at each other in simulation warfare: all happy memories of exhilarating times at the beach. Playing cards, board games, and comic book reading filled the early evening. Without electric lights, bedtime was usually early except when a beach bon fire distracted us. As an adolescent, this was sufficient entertainment. When I returned as a single adult male of twenty with overactive testosterone, the activities that fully occupied my time and attention previously seemed no longer adequate. College life had ingrained in me the need for new pursuits; most important was an understanding that "partying" was actually a verb, an action word, a goal in life, something to seek out continually. My definition of a party was anywhere one could drink in excess with the potential of meeting willing women. Life was simple at twenty.

Days off were just preludes to nights out. My internal clock had become accustomed to the cycle of noon to 2:00 a.m. as my biological awake time. Since I had grown accustomed to that time for work, it was an easy transition to the same time frame for play. I took my days off very seriously. I wanted to make good use of these hours since there was so little of them available. I often felt like wasting my "best years" when I frittered away any possibility for joining in on a good party.

Fire Island didn't suffer from a lack of potential party places, and parties were what I craved on my nights out. The other six nights of each week, I was merely an observer; I watched others having a good time and letting loose. At least one night each week, I yearned for the chance to be an active participant.

Having the taxi at my disposal was a positive advantage. It had wheels. I wasn't confined to just places I had to walk. I had nothing against walking, but the taxi allowed for exploration of the entire island, a far better arrangement. I never specifically asked Roger or Everett if I could use the cab on my nights off, but I thought it more prudent to ask forgiveness rather than permission. That way, at least it didn't disrupt my plans, and, if necessary, I would find a way to redeem myself later. I doubted they could imagine a taxi used for anything other than for business. Why cause them concern unnecessarily.

Wheels made it possible for me to be where I thought there might be some action. I was never sure what I had in mind when thinking about "action." I think I meant any occasion where a party was happening or the place where the ladies were congregating; synonyms for fun. I often got a headache when thinking too hard about where I had the best chance of getting "lucky." My personal estimate of my social life at that time was less than superlative. I thought of myself as an introvert, lacking in confidence when in the presence of other people. I did not have a group of friends with whom I regularly hung out and with whom I could always count for having something to do on days off. The friends I grew up with at Fire Island, with the exception of Buddy, left the island for summer jobs. I had no ready-made social contacts.

Each Tuesday evening was a crap shoot as to what to do and with whom to do it. That didn't deter my expectations, however. I always began my nights out with an expectation of an evening of social consequence, discovering a party to which I would be invited and hopeful that 1 would meet a willing and beautiful female who becomes completely stricken with me. The optimum word was "hopeful." The optimal possibility remained minimal.

When looking for a "good time," as I understood good times, I was not confined to any single community. Fire Island's different cultures afforded possibilities for parties at different times and places. I was sure, however, that I did not want to stay at Water Island, where my parents lived. Having no electricity contributed to the early retirement of the residents who feared that the kerosene they needed for lights would run out and not be readily available when they really needed it. Bed time and dusk coincided.

Come nine o'clock on Tuesdays just after the sun set and my fishing exploits put to rest, it was time to move out. After explaining to my mother I was going out, she replied, "But you're out every night." I took off in my cab looking for the party, the ultimate party, any party. My primary focus for the night was the hope--better yet, the intent--of getting lucky. This was not a thought I shared with my mother.

The odds were against me, however, as I did not have the temperament for being a wild party animal, nor could I claim superior expertise in the arena of social graces. Despite my grandiose intentions, I was a novice with little familiarity in making new relationships, particularly with females. For most of my adolescent years I was socially inept. Part of this I brought upon myself, a certain amount of self-loathing; a feeling that I was never adequate or able to live up to my own or others' social expectations. I longed for an assertive personality that I admired among my peers, who always seemed to be comfortable in relationships with women, particularly when meeting them for the first time. My friend Harry from Junior High school was a mentor to me. He had that ability of being particularly attractive by females, not because he was outstandingly handsome, but because he had the ability of creative gab. When Harry approached girls; it made them feel accepted and they responded positively. Harry tried to convince me that I could become socially assertive, but it never registered. Instead panic gripped me. I feared my inadequacies would quickly become evident and rejection would be forthcoming. It was more than mere bashfulness. I thought of it as a character flaw. Feeling awkward with girls caused me considerable grief, so much so that instead of instigating conversation with a girl, I lived with the anticipation, always unrealized, that I need only wait and she would instigate the conversation with me. Did this ever happen? Rarely that I can remember.

Fire Island didn't lack for night life. There were always parties somewhere; it just took some determination and persistence to locate them. With the exception of Water Island and Skunk Hollow, every community catered to the party crowd. Not all parties, however, are created equal. Nighttime amusements reflected the culture and demeanor of the community in which they were located. It depended on what type of revelry one was considering.

Pat's Place was on the dunes at Cherry Grove. It catered to gays but not exclusively. It was one of the few bars at Cherry

Grove that survived, better yet, thrived, on visitors who came to the Grove from the straight communities to join in the party atmosphere created by the gays. Each time I went, there always seemed to be a few straight women mixed in among the gay men. Noticeable absent were straight single men. If a single female was looking for a place where she could be assured that no man would hit upon her, Pat's place was the ideal. It was a safe haven for females. Gay men don't prey upon ladies.

I found the idea of straight ladies at a gay men's bar interesting. Since I recognized that I was not good at initiating conversation with females, I figured what better place to attract a single female than at a gay bar. If I were the only single straight male, my chances greatly increased. Gay men, despite being a hell of a lot more attractive than I am, offered no competition. A girl could dream, but dreams were not reality. I was reality. I figured that being a minority straight male at Pat's Place gave me special status. I was always at the ready when and if any straight female tired of the gay male mentality.

When not overwhelmed by a desire for female companionship, I often visited Pat's Place for other entertainment. By ten on any given night there was barely room to maneuver. People, mostly men, stood backside to backside, cheek to cheek, sometimes in conversion and often just eyeing each other. The French singer, Edith Piaf's soulful tunes filled the room along with the music of Carol Channing and Mary Martin.

Pats Place was where you went if being noticed was important. I went to Pat's, however, to see, to ogle. Since I wasn't gay, attracting other gays mattered little. I was intrigued. I wanted to witness the gay life-style, to see the gay fashion on parade, to watch in amazement as gay men danced with each other, listen to their conversations about the latest in clothing styles, who was "most divine" that year in the movies or on Broadway, and witness the occasional "cat fights" between gay men. They could be brutal in their insults and insinuations, but always creative.

I would mosey in trying to look inconspicuous. My

attempts at being discreet were usually met with ridicule. One night I remember I wore my usual attire into Pats, I didn't give much thought to dress codes. I wore jeans and my college sweat shirt with a logo on the front. While I was sitting at the bar, a guy approached and ordered a drink. Waiting for his drink to come, he turned toward me and blurted out, "Oh honey, don't we look gorgeous tonight." I smiled. He then took a step back and gazed at the front of my sweat shirt emblazoned with the name of my school-- Marietta College. "Marietta College," he repeated loudly, "Isn't that a Catholic girl's school?" He then burst out laughing, picked up his gin and tonic, and returned to his friends standing nearby. The whole group turned toward me and a mild chuckle erupted from the cluster.

When I needed a break or change of venue or simply wanted to be in an atmosphere more conducive to my familiar college fraternity life-style, I headed for Davis Park and its casino. If any gays frequented Davis Park, they were well closeted. Everything about Davis Park was in sharp contrast to the ethos of Cherry Grove or Fire Island Pines. It lacked culture and bordered on the rowdy. Its residents stayed put and didn't travel much to other parts of the island. I remembered the sophomoric attitude of college students of the 60's. When not marching in a civil rights parade, partying was their primary objective. It had no amenities of sophistication, no arts organizations, no home owners' improvement associations, few community-sponsored clam bakes, and no dunes protection activists. It was a transient community of renters who thrived on anonymity.

Anonymity was a key ingredient for the perfect party atmosphere. People let loose best when they knew there were no consequences, no responsibilities, no commitments, and no repercussions. Anonymity provided all four of these conditions. Parties occurred without needing a cause or reason and happened almost spontaneously. Because it was six o'clock was sufficient reason for a party.

On occasional Tuesdays, I went to Davis Park with the excuse that I needed a shower. Aunt Ethel had a hot shower at her cottage, a luxury we didn't have at Water Island.

After a week of accumulated crusted salt on my body, I began to feel as if entombed in concrete. Precisely at 6:00 p.m. my Uncle Harvey and I, along with a pitcher of mixed Manhattan cocktails, would begin our round of "sixish" gatherings. These began between five and seven each evening. They were informal events but hardly spontaneous, that happened just about anywhere two boardwalks crossed. People would gather intentionally, some of whom you might have met previously and others as complete strangers, but not for long. People acted as if they accidentally showed up. They just happened to have with them a pitcher of Manhattans, or bottle of gin and two bottles of tonic, or a container of premixed Whiskey Sours along with a few appropriate glasses. These were no-beer affairs. All that was required was a few people, a boardwalk to sit on, and sufficient alcohol to induce inebriation. Almost every corner or set of steps or front deck or empty patch of sand was fair game for a "sixish" gathering. No invitations needed. Just show up.

My Uncle Harvey, Aunt Ethel's husband, was very much the impish type. He enjoyed a good party or a bad party; made no difference to him as long as it passed as a party. I considered it imperative that Uncle Harvey go with me, or I with him, to whatever "sixish" party was happening that evening. He was my medium. We worked as a team. Uncle Harvey had a very gregarious, almost mischievous personality, one that attracted people like flies to sugar. He had lines for the ladies like I had never heard before. Without a blink, he would address a complete stranger with the most personal requests. He told a lady she was very pretty and then, almost in the same breath, ask her "Will you spend the night with me?" Some of his lines were classics like, "Are you an interior decorator? Cause when I saw you, the room became beautiful" or "Are you religious? Cause you're the answer to all my prayer." I remember his favorite. "I'm not drunk, I'm just intoxicated by you."

Because of his age (about 60) and the tone in which he spoke these comments, he was never taken seriously or considered offensive, but rather thought to be cute, witty, and charming. Aunt Ethel, at the very least, tolerated his behavior. It was always our strategy that once he struck up a conversation with a female and had her attention, he would look toward me and I would indicate with a nod if I were interested. He intentionally chose ladies that he felt were age appropriate for me, as he knew, or resigned himself to understand, that he was not actually in the market for himself. When our eyes met, we easily communicated positively or negatively. That was our sign. Uncle Harvey then showered his charm upon the unsuspecting lady with a few of his most appealing and charismatic lines and then directed her attention toward me

"My nephew over there drives a taxi on the beach. Ever been for a taxi ride on the beach? It's really romantic. I'm sure he wouldn't mind taking you down to the Grove this evening. I'd go along myself with you, but I have to get back to my wife. She really misses me when I'm gone too long and it's way past my bedtime"

We both then stopped talking and waited to see what the lady's response would be. If there was any positive rejoinder, even the slightest hint that she was interested, he would introduce her to me. If not, we would try again on another unsuspecting attractive female. It was a strategy that I conjured up due to my own introversion in the hope of meeting girls; who I felt held great potential. Unfortunately, I don't remember a single time that things worked out as planned.

I had much better luck as a party crasher. Through the Davis Park grapevine, no house party was a secret for very long. Word spread quickly. Once I learned of a prospective house party, I invited myself. Despite my introversion, I found it was easy. I arrived at the house and introduced myself.

"Hi, I'm a friend of the renter," I would say, studiously avoiding the renter's name which I did not know. That ploy seemed to always work since the actual renter of the house was usually not present, and those renting the house were sub leasers. More than likely, half the groupers renting the house didn't know the other half. These were loosely affiliated relationships. Groups might not even be friends, but joined in partnership with people from the same or neighboring office in renting a house for two weeks. Only a few from the group were in residence at any one time, so they couldn't identify or remember all the others in the rental arrangement. I could have said I was one of the actual renters and have been just as accepted. I was welcomed to the party, but because of my inability to make easy conversation with strangers, I often left before making new friends or getting lucky. I just couldn't find a comfortable demeanor among people I met at Davis Park parties.

When all else failed, I pinned my hopes on the casino. The Davis Park casino, built at minimal cost and probably by the lowest bidder, had passed its prime at least a decade before. Shingles were falling off the sides, it needed a paint job, the back side sagged, and locust posts propped up the entire building. Inside was a small snack bar with a limited supply of stale snacks and ice cream that remained only partially frozen. The dining room felt like a cross between a Howard Johnson restaurant and a Mama's Café. The food attractively advertised on the menu turned out to be franchise food served lukewarm on paper plates with plastic utensils.

The big attraction at the casino was the bar. If it wasn't the only bar at Davis Park, it wouldn't have been an attraction at all. A large horseshoe-shaped bar covered nearly half the room. Barstools were limited. The wooden floor, used for dancing to juke box tunes, was pulling apart with nails protruding. The casino was the location of last resort for those who failed to hook up with someone earlier in the evening, the last chance café, so to speak. After the sixish affairs and the house parties, if you showed up at the casino, you were marked as a loser, at least for that night.

Week day nights were my only opportunity to visit the casino. I always went with great expectations, but disappointment was the usual outcome. I had terrible bar expertise. I think the root of my problem was my essential shyness and timidity, combined with my fear of rejection. I longed for the ability and skill to be able to freely initiate a conversation with someone new, someone I wanted to meet. But when fear gripped me, I got tongue-tied and morphed into my solitude. Conversing wasn't the problem. Under different circumstances I did well when conversation wasn't forced and wasn't an indicator of social aptitude like in a classroom describing the essentials of the Magna Carta or in a meeting planning for a fraternity party. These conversations didn't reveal social proficiency; they had a different purpose and there was no expectancy of first impressions. But in a bar, especially with females, I had no opening lines, no sense of social know how, no confidence that I had anything interesting to present. I felt more at ease responding to someone who approached me, but who was I kidding? That wasn't going to happen.

Not all was a lost cause. At one of the restaurants at Fire Island Pines, where I went for take-out food, a dark curly-haired girl served food from behind the counter. I found her attractive, partly because of her looks and partly because she talked to me. She initiated conversation. For my part, I could muster a "Can I have another Pepsi?" or "How much do I owe you for the hamburger?" But in addition to answering my requests, she initiated more. "How do you like driving the taxi?" and "Where do you go to college?" I immediately interpreted her response as indicating an interest in me. I wanted to reciprocate. It was time to ask her out.

It had been many months, probably my last semester at college, since I had asked a girl out. Notice I say "asked," not "went on a date." The other drivers took notice of my interest. They pieced together why I drank six Pepsis each afternoon, each one requiring that I pay a visit to the snack bar and linger longer than necessary. They urged me to ask her out; more than an urging, it was a challenge. It was either ask her out, or face the consequences of an unending mocking from the drivers that I was the world's worst wimp and without balls for failing to follow through. I felt forced to make the proposal but was not altogether unwilling.

"Would you like to go with me to Flynns on Tuesday?" I blurted out just as she handed me my seventh Pepsi of the day.

"You mean this Tuesday like tomorrow?"

"Is tomorrow Tuesday?" That was unrehearsed and sounded as if I lacked the ability to absorb what day of the week it was or maybe even my own name. "Yeah. That's good. That okay with you?"

"Yes. Okay," she said. I waited a moment expecting the inevitable "but I can't" to come from her. I was mentally preparing to offer another time or maybe a different place or to say, "Well maybe some other day." Her "yes" caught me off guard. I choked on my swallow of Pepsi.

"You okay?" she asked.

"Yeah fine," I wiped the soda from my chin with my sleeve. Another smooth move, surely one to impress her. "Why don't I pick you up here at nine? We can use my taxi to get to Flynns."

The next night I didn't fish after supper. I thought the odor of fish bait would follow me the remainder of the night. Instead I drove the short distance to Aunt Ethel's house for my weekly shower. I had one clean set of clothes that I had brought for when I left the Island for the trip home in September; a pair of white chinos and a tee shirt with an emblem of the New York Yankees stenciled on the front. I thought this a more appropriate moment to wear them than to save for a car trip. I put them on, feeling a bit over dressed for Fire Island.

I arrived at Fire Island Pines precisely at nine. Timing seemed to consume my attention. While never feeling compelled to be prompt while driving the taxi, this night was one of first impressions. I wanted to be on time to show my maturity, responsibility, and respect.

We met outside the snack bar where she worked. She looked gorgeous. She wore a flowered print dress, and carried her sandals in her hand. She looked unbelievably fresh and neat. I felt embarrassed that I hadn't cleaned out the inside of my cab. I offered excuses and apologies, but she graciously declined the need.

We drove the six miles from the Pines to Ocean Bay Park. What conversation we had was limited and consisted of questions about what we did in between summers. She went to college, an all-girl school in northern New York State.

There was a cut in the dunes just west of the center of Ocean Bay Park that allowed us to drive into the village and park alongside Flynns on the bay front. Flynns bordered the high wire fence that surrounded the neighboring Point O' Woods community. I remember we ambled over to the fence and peered inside and wondered together whether they meant to fence people out or fence them in.

I chose Flynns because I liked its laid-back, eclectic feel. From times I had been there previously, its assortment of clientele greatly impressed me for its diversity. Gays and straights, married and singles, blacks and whites, old and young, all seemed to mingle well, giving the place an air of being cosmopolitan and honky-tonk at the same time. Music was as likely to be country/western as jazz or rock-and-roll.

At one time the Flynns building had been part of the Fire Island Life Saving Service. Tradition has it that boats and equipment was stored there. It was an unpretentious edifice, resembling a large barn hanging over the water's edge. It looked like it had been partially restored using driftwood found along the beachfront. No two pieces of siding matched in color. Cracks existed between planks. Its floor was also wooden plank. It had no windows, only shutters that opened by pulling on ropes. Paint was peeling or completely nonexistent. The deck overhanging the shallow water of the bay was drooping, and the railing, meant to prevent drunks from falling into the water, was dilapidated. I suspected they kept the building in its present condition out of a feeling for nostalgia demanded by the many repeat customers who had patronized the facility for decades. I think I remember my parents' talking about visiting Flynns that one summer they rented a house there while I was very young. Besides, it relied on its reputation as a meeting place for party goers, not its ambiance, for its economic survival.

We sat at a table inside near the dance floor. It was too cool to be outside, I thought. There was no service. I went to the bar and brought back two beers. She sipped hers slowly. I drank mine ferociously. I was still quite nervous. I went and got a second beer. On the way back, I stopped at the juke box and fed some quarters into the machine. I pressed all the Ray

Charles tunes I knew, choosing "I Can't Stop Loving You" at least three times. I asked if she wanted to dance. She didn't answer, but got up and received my outstretched hand. We were the only ones dancing, but it felt comfortable, as no one stared at us. I started to relax.

We each had another beer and danced a second time when my favorite Ray Charles tune played again. My confidence was building, enough so that words, even whole sentences, and some that made sense, came from my mouth. She paid attention and seemed genuinely interested in what I had to say. I rambled on and on, surprising myself that I could actually keep a conversation going with a girl.

"Enough about me," I told her. I started to ask her questions, personal things about her job, her school, her plans for her future, and how she felt about gays. My fraternity brothers coached me that women like personal questions. It helps convince them that not all men are egotistical. I was fishing for connections. I was really hoping to get lucky.

She seemed reticent at first to talk about herself. Then, almost spontaneously, she leaned toward me and looked directly at me. "You should know," she said. "I'm on the rebound." She looked very serious as if she were telling me she had some sort of transmittable sexual disease. Her brows furrowed as if she were deep in thought. I wasn't sure, but by the look on her face, I knew it was serious.

"What do you mean on the rebound?" I asked.

"From my boyfriend," she said. 'The guy I've been dating got himself into some trouble. Something about some fights he was in. Now he's on probation. I told him I didn't want to be around him when he acted like that. We haven't seen each other for a few weeks now." She confessed that she still liked him and had feelings for him and found it difficult to say to him that she wanted to break up. She wasn't sure she could get over him easily. She didn't think he was over the relationship either, as he has called her repeatedly over the past few weeks. "He does have a temper that gets him into trouble," she added.

Her revelation immediately put me on the defensive. I suddenly felt as if I was interfering some place where I ought not to be. I began to think that perhaps I was being used, just another form of rejection. Her confession was her way of letting me down slowly. I wondered, however, who this person might be.

"What's his name?" I asked

"Jay," he said. "Jay McCloud."

A light dawned in my consciousness. A very bright and scary light. "You mean Jay McCloud, Jerry's brother?" I asked.

"Yeah. Do you know him?'

"Uh...No. But I have heard about him. I know Jerry. Jerry drives weekends for White Cap."

"Oh yeah," she said. "I forgot."

It took only a flash of a second for me to recall some of the tales of trouble I had heard about Jay McCloud. He had been in fights at Cherry Grove and Davis Park. It seems that he and some of his cronies drank too much and became inebriated, which was almost every weekend, and came over to the island just itching for trouble. He had a reputation for gay bashing, but not exclusively. He wasn't particular about his fights; anyone who pissed him off was eligible. This last time, it took a half dozen police who came to the island in boats just to arrest him, so the story goes. I didn't risk telling her I knew these tales nor did I mention his reputation, especially not right after she told me he was her boyfriend. Sometimes I am slow but not stupid.

The urge to say "whoa" and step back from this budding relationship suddenly seemed paramount for safety reasons alone. The consequences--a severe beating by a psycho and his band of hooligans--of pursuing a relationship with the girlfriend of a reputable madman caused sweat to bead on my forehead. It was clearly time to go and I needed an excuse.

"Roger wants to work on this taxi (that was a lie) the first thing tomorrow morning. Maybe we best get going, since I got to show up early in the morning sober." I was already feeling anxious and a bit paranoid. I glanced around Flynns looking for anyone with an interest in watching us. I suspected she caught a hint of my fear as she watched me wipe sweat from my brow despite it being a cool evening.

She was too polite to say anything. She didn't offer any resistance to my suggestion that it was time to leave.

We exited Flynns through a side door. I went out first, nearly knocking her down as I attempted to look both ways from the doorway. It now felt like a clandestine affair, a secret rendezvous that I was trying to keep hidden. Anonymity was a priority. My sudden fear turned to uneasiness. I hurried her into the cab and shut the doors. Paranoia was gaining on me.

We arrived back at the Pines at a different spot from where I picked her up. I didn't get out of the cab but instead reached across her lap and opened her door from the inside. I had no thoughts then about groping her or seeking a good night kiss. As pleasant and as pretty as she was, it wasn't sufficient motivation to keep my mind from thinking about her boyfriend catching me in her company. I wanted to put distance between us as soon as possible. I imagined her having thoughts about what a jerk I must be, a real wimp with no compassion or empathy, but that would have to be resolved another day. The thought that she was Jay McCloud's girlfriend had to remain my primary motivation for moving on. I had thoughts that it would be nice to share with her that she wasn't a pariah to be shunned, but that I had to take my own bodily safety into consideration. It was unfair to her, but perhaps someday in a different location I would be able to explain my behavior. Right now I wanted to stay healthy with my body unblemished.

I did see her again, frequently, but from a distance. I stayed on the other side of the counter when ordering my Pepsi's and hamburgers. She was polite and considerate as if she fully understood my predicament. My conversation was limited but cordial. I continued, however, to be plagued by fears that behind that telephone pole down by the dock or lurking in the dark outside the office, or perhaps surprising me sitting in the front seat of my cab upon my return from going to the bathroom, would be either Jay or one of his friends waiting to jump on me to deliver a severe beating for "messing" with his girlfriend. I never did confront Jay and was happy at not having the opportunity. It would have been extremely awkward trying to convince him that I had no intentions with his girlfriend after I had already taken her out. He would never have believed that, not for a moment.

Days off and nights out, they never seemed to live up to expectations. My thoughts that having transportation on Fire Island, certainly an advantage for exploring the many communities, would also provide me with an abundance of friends, particularly female, never panned out. Needless to say a 1955 Willy's Jeep is not a suitable substitute for a Corvette.

15

A Matter of Seniority

Thousands of words are written about the origin of the name (Jeep). Many believe that the name came from the corruption of the U.S. Army acronym GP, for general purpose. Then there is the Popeye strip cartoon. Eugene the jeep was a small, impish animal that had the power to solve all sorts of problems and which was featured in the Popeye cartoon strip created by E.C. Segar in 1936.

--Courtesy of Daimler Chrysler ASG

At White Cap Taxi, seniority mattered to drivers. There was a clearly defined pecking order. Factors that seemed to sometimes defy logic or reason determined which jeep you got to drive. Everett or Roger assigned each driver a taxi. There were a few times when they disagreed, and the driver was left in limbo without a jeep until these two worked out their differences. Most times seniority determined status; a matter of how many years one worked for White Cap. Status dictated which jeep the owners assigned to each driver. Those with status got the best of the taxis. Like the young urban professional who seeks the corner office as a sign of rank and prestige, of utmost importance to drivers was to which jeep they were entrusted.

Other factors also came into play. Both Roger and Everett held a bias against college students. Their opinion was that "higher learning" only confused one's sense of responsibility, and college students were the most confused of all. College clouded the ability to make good decisions. All that fraternity partying, the drinking, and the free sex had confused their minds and obstructed their ability to make sound judgments. Hence, college students got the most decrepit of the jeeps, the ones that barely held together.

A few drivers didn't fit either of the above circumstances. They neither had longevity, nor were they ignored because they attended college. These drivers tended to be high school dropouts who worked during the week as carpenters or plumbers. Because they held "real "jobs and were often married, Roger's estimation of them was they had earned some status as a result of maturity. He esteemed them way above the students and just a little below those with who had worked with him many years. Their assignment of taxis took priority over the lowly college student. The most important element in assigning taxis, however, remained the discretion of the owners, which wasn't always fair, consistent, or reasonable. But what the hell, they owned the jeeps.

Just as there was differing status among drivers, so also was there among jeeps. Not all jeeps were equal. Perhaps they were created equal, but time and circumstances, combined with abuse and neglect, took a toll on the condition of the vehicles. Some taxis were less desirable than others were. They all looked similar: red boxy bodies, four wheels, a large tailgate, and a white roof, but great disparities existed. Some had badly worn interiors. Some radios were less functional. The number of dents, scratches and missing paint spots often determined the age of the vehicle. Older taxis had less power and appeared less inviting to ride in. None of the jeeps were in picture-perfect condition, all shiny and clean and smelling fresh, but the looks of the jeep were less important in determining status than other factors

Of greatest importance to drivers was the size of the engine. Most had four cylinder engines: adequate power but lacking in get-up and go in soft sand. The newer jeeps had six cylinder engines, generating greatly more power. The greater the power, the swifter the speed; the swifter the speed, the quicker the arrival at the destination. How did this matter? When two drivers were competing for the same fare, it was a matter of first come, first served.

More privileged drivers moved up to six cylinders. Ralph, an older man who only drove on weekends, and employed by the owners since they first started the taxi service, held the highest esteem. Despite being a weekend driver, he had the quickest, most powerful, and newest of the six-cylinder jeeps. Clearly Ralph had the highest status. I envied him. Someday, I hoped, I would get Ralph's jeep if I just worked hard, got out of college, or whenever Ralph entered that spot in heaven for used-up taxi drivers, whichever came first.

The cream of the crop, the Cadillac of the White Cap fleet, was the fully charged and ultimately powerful eight-cylinder International Harvester. It was huge, in prime condition, and fairly new (maybe 5-6 years old). Roger kept a firm grip on who got to drive the International. Usually no one except himself and Everett, the other owner, ever had access to it. I think Roger brought the International to the beach for the primary reason of keeping the seniority system intact. He needed a goal toward which drivers were willing to work. The International was probably out of reach to the lowly college student driver; nonetheless it held the highest esteem as the ultimate reward for loyal service.

It was never stated, but I became convinced that the real criteria for seniority for taxi drivers was actually fairly simple and based on proven scientific evidence. Roger and Everett declared that anybody under the age of twenty-five, and in college, had to be irresponsible and needed an older four-cylinder jeep. Anybody more than forty-five or married was mature and responsible and was entitled to a six-cylinder jeep. Despite my previous categorizing of driver status, the primary emphasis seemed more focused on age and lack of education. There didn't seem to be any other criteria for the seniority system other than both owners held college students in contempt, thought them too young and reckless, and considered them basically idiots

I drove one of the four-cylinder jeeps the first year that I worked, and never graduated beyond four-cylinders. I never made it past the under twenty-five, foolishly reckless, considerably irresponsible, and idiot criteria.

Near the end of my last year driving for White Cap Taxi, my ancient Willys had a breakdown, partially mechanical and, I suspect, partially emotional. It became very temperamental and reacted bitterly when I used foul language to describe its many shortcomings. It kept over-heating which I attributed to a mental lapse due to sheer exhaustion. I drove it unmercifully. Roger diagnosed it differently. He said it had a small leak in the radiator.

"You don't need to worry about it if you do what I say," Roger told me one day as I complained about it not running right. "Carry this here jug of water with you all the time and when you see the thermostat needle going up, stop and put water in it, you hear?"

"Yea, I hear. But what if the leak gets bigger and you know that's gonna happen just before a big weekend? The Fourth of July is coming soon." I was worried that I wouldn't have a taxi to drive for one of the biggest money-making holidays.

"Just keep water in it and stop bitching. Worrying never got you anything. But it's your ass if you don't do like I tell you and keep it full of water." Roger was always so reassuring.

The jug was full of water and positioned under the front seat. There it stayed without being disturbed for days. Other things distracted me; things like eating, showering, being tired, and girls with bikinis. I forget to check the radiator gauge. On Friday morning, the day before the Fourth of July weekend, I noticed water on the sand under the motor as I was getting into the jeep. I remembered Roger's mandate, but it was too late. When I looked in the radiator, it was empty. No problem. I'll just fill it with water. When it was full and the jug was empty, I started the engine. Just as it turned over, I saw a stream of water gushing out the front of the jeep. Within a few seconds, the engine came to a halt. Steam was now ushering from under the engine compartment. The radiator had sprung a leak, a very large leak.

My first thought was I had to get the jeep to Roger as soon as possible. My second, thought causing great consternation, was that Roger was going to be pissed. He warned me beforehand how I could have avoided the problem. This would only confirm his belief that most college boys were basic idiots with little or no regard for following directions. To right the situation, I filled a half dozen water jugs from the pump at my house and stashed them in the jeep. I then took off for the Pines. With frequent stops every half mile or so and by continuously refilling the radiator, I managed to limp along the beach until I reached Fire Island Pines.

"You didn't watch the water level and now you're shit out of luck," Roger said. It was just about what I expected him to say.

I took a chance that I could avoid blame by saying to Roger, "You knew it was bad. Why didn't we get it fixed before it was a problem?" I waited for Roger to go into one of his full-blown yelling fits about how irresponsible and reckless you kids are under twenty-five, especially when they go to college.

He didn't explode. "You know," he admitted, "I got this radiator from a junk yard last winter. It didn't look too good when Everett put it in. I think I'll bring it back to the junk yard and look for a different one." His reaction completely surprised me. I immediately recognized, however, that this procedure would take at least a week, if not longer. I might still have a job, but without a taxi, it didn't really matter.

At first, Roger made no mention of me driving anything, much less another jeep. There weren't any others available. All the weekend drivers were due later this day and they would want their own jeeps.

With what little audacity I could muster, I asked, "So what am I supposed to do now? I got nothing to drive." I half-expected Roger to say, "Tough shit, not my problem." But I also knew that if I didn't drive, Roger wouldn't get his sixty percent of my fares. I reminded him. "You know, if I lose money this weekend, so do you."

Roger was silent for a few minutes while he started to

unbolt the radiator from my jeep. Then he stood up, wiped his hands on his pants and said, "Use my International until Monday."

Did I hear right? Did Roger actually say, "Use the International until Monday?"

"Here's the key," he said, digging in his pants pocket. "Make sure you have *enougha* gas and don't even think about getting it wet or stuck in the soft sand."

Roger's trust caught me completely by surprise, and for a moment I felt euphoric. "I won't. I'll treat it like it was my own taxi," I said. I sounded like a child who just had his greatest Christmas wish come true, a live pony under the tree. It was probably the wrong thing to say at that moment, having just thoroughly mistreated my own taxi. Roger just looked at me then went back to unbolting the radiator.

The International. Eight cylinders. Big enough to fit ten people inside. I started the day at the bottom of the seniority scale (under twenty-five, a college student, irresponsible, and reckless) and now I have the ultimate driving machine, the ultimate status symbol in all of Taxidom--the International eight cylinder taxi. I couldn't believe my luck. It felt like a dream from which I was about to awaken. Not only was I not in Roger's shit house, but I seemed to be in his good graces, forgiven and rewarded. I wasted no time leaving the Pines before Roger changed his mind.

My first trip was down to Cherry Grove. The fare I carried--six people--weren't as impressed with the International as I was; just another taxi ride for them. But when I reached the Grove and the other drivers saw me in the Roger's Cadillac, I knew I had some explaining to do, along with some gloating

"How come you got the International?"

"Mine's broken," I said. "It's got a blown radiator. Roger is letting me use this until Monday."

"Yea sure," one driver replied. You must be doing a lot of ass kissing."

"I'll bet you sabotaged your jeep yourself," another driver said. The jealousy was clearly apparent already.

About two in the morning I decided to call it quits for the night. I told the office I was going home. On the ride back toward Water Island, the tide was low and the sand flat and hard along the water's edge. All eight cylinders went straight to my head. I pushed the International into third gear and clocked out at forty-five miles per hour. The engine was just humming along, so I dropped down into fourth gear. It was a nice smooth ride. Too nice a ride to quit now, I thought to myself. I reached Water Island in about fifteen minutes. Before I had time to think what I was doing, I drove right by doing about fifty miles an hour.

Water Island was behind me now. I was fast approaching Davis Park, the next community two miles to the east. Lights were still on in the houses along the beach-front, and a few couples were walking the beach. By now, I had no thoughts of turning around. Why not go all the way to Smith Point? It can't be more than about ten miles. It's such a nice night and with eight cylinders, I'll be back in less than half an hour.

Past Davis Park I saw no lights at all except for the moon reflecting off the surface of the ocean. The furthermost east end of the island tended to be isolated with the exception of Long Cove and Skunk Hollow, both rather skimpy communities of fishermen and clamdiggers who go to bed early. I reached Smith Point where the beach begins to run out and there is a road over the dune that connects to a bridge off the Island. I crossed the parking lot and headed over the bridge. I had thoughts of driving all the way to Patchogue on the mainland and stopping to see if my cousin, Harvey, was home yet and wanted to go for a ride. But I hesitated. My eye caught the gas gauge on the dashboard. It was on empty. Empty? How empty? How long had it been on empty? Why didn't I think to look before? Stupid mistake.

Maybe it has a reserve tank for emergencies just like the one I confronted now. I was twenty miles from home in Roger's International at two thirty in the morning. Not where I am supposed to be.

My only thought was to start back toward Water Island and hope for the best. If the gauge had been on empty for some time, I was in real trouble. If it just got to the empty, my chances of making the fifteen miles or so looked pretty good. I trusted my luck and kept the International down on the hard sand in fourth gear. I figured if the gas ran out, I could coast a few hundred yards if I was going fast enough. I got to Blue Point with no trouble. Just as I passed the old Coast Guard Station with about one mile to go, the engine started coughing. I let up on the accelerator to use as little gas as possible. I made it to Water Island on fumes. A sigh of relief overcame me as I sat there for a moment before heading into the house. I dreaded the next day having to call Roger to tell him I was out of gas.

The next morning, I hunted for any gas I could find around our house, but nothing turned up. My friend Buddy and his family had left the Island for a week so they would not be a source of help. I sat in the cab for a while thinking about my alibi. No new thoughts occurred. Then about a mile down the beach, I spotted a White Cap Taxi heading my way. Who could that be? If it was Everett, it would be worse than if it was Roger. Everett's temper was notorious. When the jeep got closer, I flagged it down. It was Ralph, the older more responsible driver who had seniority and a six-cylinder cab. Ralph stopped, and I shared my predicament. I didn't offer any explanations, and he didn't ask for any.

"You don't have a siphon tube or anything like that, do you Ralph? I asked.

"No but it just so happens that I do have a gallon of gas in the back," Ralph responded. "I always carry an extra can in case I run out." He said that with a tone of sarcasm that meant I had better do the same thing.

"It's best that you not tell Roger I ran out of gas with his International. He'll blow a fuse." Ralph didn't ask any questions.

We poured the gas in my International's tank, started the engine and we both left for Fire Island Pines. Now I knew why Roger insisted on the seniority system.

16

Unlucky

*Lesbian existence comprises both the breaking of a taboo
and the rejection of a compulsory way of life. It is also
a direct or indirect attack on the male right of access to
women.*

--Adrienne Rich

She had been in my cab a few times before. I didn't think
of her as particularly attractive but certainly not ugly. I knew
she was older than I was, but she had a certain demeanor
that made her seem sensual, at least in my meager opinion.

It was late on a Thursday night as I remember it. I was
waiting in my cab at the usual pickup place at the Grove. It
was about the time we usually brought people home after
a night of partying, back to where we first picked them up.
I was in line, and since it was a slow night for business, the
few drivers working agreed to take turns with returning
customers. I was first in line.

She came down the steps and walked toward my cab. I
remember she wore a halter top, the kind that draped off her
shoulders, scarcely covering her breasts. Around her waist
she had tied a flimsy skirt, very thin, the kind that looked
like it was silk as it waved in the breeze exposing her legs.
Even in the dim light I could see the sun bronzed her well.

After my disastrous stint with the cute girl with the
frizzy brown hair with the psycho boyfriend, I hadn't

done much female pursuing. That incident had shaken my confidence; deflated my self-esteem. I still carried fears that any female companionship without discretion might elicit dire consequences; cause me to further regard myself as a loser. The urge, however, I tucked securely in the back of my mind, ready to emerge at the slightest stimulation. For the meantime, the motivation was well under control, and I was feeling more laid back and not so harried to get lucky. Besides, summer was coming to an end shortly, as Labor Day was approaching. I tried focusing on school to alleviate distressful social symptoms.

She walked up beside my cab and stood staring at me without speaking. I stared back for a moment, regained my composure, and said, "You need a cab to get back home?"

"Yes," she said. "Yes I do."

"Jump in," I told her.

She shuffled around to the other side of the cab and opened the passenger side door. It surprised me, as I thought she would get in the back seat. She slid into the front seat beside me.

"Where are we going?" I asked. I don't usually ask were *we* are going, but rather where do *you* want to go. It just slipped out spontaneously. Of course, as her driver, I would be going there also, but *"we"* sounded more subjective as if *we* were going together. At that moment it just felt right.

"Back to Davis Park," she told me.

I think she saw the scowl on my face, again a spontaneous gesture that seemed to always appear whenever I heard "back to Davis Park." I knew immediately that it would be a long ride, take considerable time, and provide no return fare. None of the drivers relished fares to Davis Park for the same reasons.

"What's the problem?" she asked. "Don't you know where Davis Park is?"

"No problem," I said.

"Then why the scowl, the sour look you gave me?"

I could smell booze on her breath, but her attentiveness surprised me. Rarely were inebriated customers aware of much at this time of night, surely not so alert so as to recognize somebody's feelings by a facial expression. Her recognition invited a response from me.

"It's just me," I said. "Usually fares to Davis Park don't happen often. It's kinda out of the way so when one of us gets a fare down there, we usually balk, or at the very least mutter under our breaths about having to go to Siberia. But I'm sorry. I'd be happy to take you there."

"Good, because that's where my house is." It was a frank statement but hard to decipher if said sarcastically or as a reassurance that no disrespect was taken.

I turned the cab around and headed east toward Davis Park. The tide was high, so driving on the packed surface near the surf was not possible. I stayed up in the soft sand by the base of the dunes. The ride would take considerably longer.

"You been driving this cab long?" she asked me. She initiated the conversation.

"Been driving each summer for the past three years."

"You look too young for this to be your full-time permanent job."

"Yeah, I do it only during the summer to earn money for school." I wanted to avoid idle conversation. I didn't feel really prepared for talking much. It was after midnight and I had been driving most of the day, but she seemed intent upon continuing.

"So you go to school, huh? What school do you go to? I suspect you're not still in high school."

"No, I'm in college, graduate school actually." I was beginning to warm up to her a bit. She sounded genuinely interested and not just making idle conversation. My mind began to take notice. This was one of the few times a female initiated conversation with me and sounded like she wanted to prolong it, at least for the meantime. Was this leading somewhere I wasn't expecting?

Her next question presented a dilemma. "Oh, graduate school, that's interesting. What are you studying?"

I knew if I told the truth, it might stall her sudden interest in me. I needed to side step this question. Telling her I was a ministerial student would be like jamming the brakes on a runaway truck or, at the very least, taking the conversation in an unwanted direction. If a liaison was possible, I wanted it to stay at a superficial level, one that didn't commit to any intellectual dialogue that would dampen a physical attraction. The longer I was in her presence, the more attractive she became. Either I was becoming more observant or it was her interest in me that was appealing. The fact that she was actually sitting next to me and we were heading together toward her home late at night caused a sudden appreciation that all things might be possible.

"I'm hoping to be a psychologist," I told her. It was as close to the truth as I dared risk without letting my chances completely slip away. It was perilous but better than telling her she was in the presence of a budding minister. I had often witnessed strange reactions to that acknowledgment.

"I have several friends who are psychologists," she told me.

Hearing that, I thought I was in trouble. What if she knew more about psychology than I did and started questioning me, a graduate student supposedly majoring in psychology, about theories I was expected to know about but didn't. That might be worse than telling the truth about my studies. Knowledgeable friends advised me often that women hate it when they catch men intentionally telling lies just to make themselves seem more attractive to females.

"Well, I'm just getting started so I don't know much about psychology, but it does sound interesting," I told her. This sounded innocuous enough. I was hoping it would end that part of the conversation. It worked.

She remained quiet for the next few minutes as we approached Davis Park.

"My house is right on the dunes, just past the casino," she said. "Up there with the porch light on."

I pulled up close to the steps leading up the dunes toward her house, a flat-roofed modern structure perched along the leading edge of the dunes.

"It's not really my house; we are just renting it for a few weeks, One of the ladies I work with shares the rent with me. She's gone this week and some friends of mine are staying with me but their still back at the Grove."

My immediate response, but unsaid, was this was an invitation of sorts. I began to think about what to say next to encourage her, but needed not say anything. She continued on her own.

"I don't know if you're allowed," she said, "since you're working now, but if you can help me up the stairs I'd appreciate it. Seems like I had a little too much to drink and I'm feeling a bit wobbly."

She must have carried her liquor real well because I had forgotten about the smell when she first entered the cab. Her conversation since then did not reveal any inebriation. I accepted the invitation.

"No problem. I'd be happy to help." I already had visions that once I got her to her house, it would feel almost natural to follow her inside under the pretension of making sure she was all right. I felt I was getting about as close as I had ever been of late to getting lucky, I did not want to let this opportunity pass. Maybe she was a bit older than I was, but her interest in me during the short ride home had stimulated my hormones almost to the breaking point.

I parked the jeep and shut off the engine. The only light came from her deck lamp. I got out of the driver's seat and stood in the sand. She remained seated. It dawned on me that she was waiting for me to go to her side of the taxi and open the passenger door. I quickly obliged. She tripped while getting out of the cab and fell into my arms. It was a natural reaction to catch her and hold her up until she steadied herself. I smelled her perfumed hair as her head cradled against my chest. She started giggling.

"I'm so sorry. I guess the booze is catching up on me."

"I'm just glad I was here to catch you," I replied. We stood still for a moment staring at each other

She broke the silence. "Since it feels like I need some help, wanna help me up to the house?"

I felt like an answer was not needed. I grabbed her arm, steadied her, and started to guide her up the stairs. We reached the top without incident and headed toward the front deck door.

You're coming in with me, aren't you?"

Again, I didn't feel obliged to talk but rather followed her inside as if I belonged there. I was thinking this all felt really good because I was not the one pursuing the encounter; didn't have to use any "come on" lines, just followed her lead like a little puppy.

"You want something to drink?" she asked when we first got in the door. "I got some cognac that's open."

Yeah, that would be nice."

"You don't have to go back to driving right away do you?"

"No, I'm pretty much done for the night".

I couldn't believe what I was hearing. It felt like I was dreaming. So little effort on my part. The invitations from her just kept coming. This felt like a completely new experience for me. I began to think that maybe I wasn't ready for this, or perhaps what I expected was not what she intended. She was, after all, a lot older than I was and more mature. Could this be the culmination of all my dreams of the ideal summer job; was I about to get lucky, and with a mature lady?

I watched as she walked toward her liquor shelf. She removed a bottle of cognac, picked up two glasses and walked back toward the couch were I was sitting. My eyes focused intently upon her body. She was not petite, but small. Very shapely, I thought. I suspect that my imagination was beginning to get the better of me because she seemed much more attractive the longer the time I spent with her. I recognized that I was less attracted to her looks and more attracted to the possibility of getting lucky, despite her looks. She sat down of the couch next to me and offered me a glass.

I began to sip the cognac, but soon found myself guzzling it. It tasted terrible. The anticipation of where this encounter might lead caused me to want to get a bit high as soon as possible .

"So tell me something about you," she asked,

"Like what do you want to know?"

"Well you look like a bright young man. What do you like to do when you are not driving the taxi?"

I was still sober enough to know I didn't want to let on I read theological literature. I also didn't want to admit to a preoccupation for chasing women, surf fishing alone, and fantasizing about parties I never attended. I surely did not want to go – intellectual. Actually, talk was not my first priority. I attempted to side step the issue.

"I'm really not that bright," I told her. I wasn't directing the conversation, but only responding as innocently as I could to her questions. I really didn't want to admit to what I was really thinking. I didn't want to talk.

She wouldn't let up. "Do you, or maybe your parents, own a house here on the island"?

"We got a cottage down at Water Island. Been in the family a long time, but it's pretty much mine now." Her question suggested that maybe she thought of me as still a child of my parents living off them, and I wanted to come off as more mature, more like a self-sufficient adult. "It's pretty much mine now" sounded to me like I was a home owner myself.

We each had another cognac. It still tasted bad, but was beginning to give me a better buzz. I began feeling less self-conscious and more confident. She noticed that I was occasionally staring at her breasts. I was.

"My breasts are my best feature," she blurted out.

I was used to talking about the size of breasts, usually with other students' at my fraternity house; never with a strange female. It caught me by surprise. I had no words of response. I immediately stopped staring. I moved closer to her on the couch. Clearly now, I could feel my juices beginning to boil. There seemed little I could do to stop it. I wanted to avoid any more talk, so I leaned into her and kissed her on the cheek. She didn't pull away, but neither did she reciprocate. I then put my arm around her shoulder in an effort to pull her closer. She responded by sitting with her backside braced against my chest. I could look over her shoulder straight down at her breasts. The feeling of reaching down and holding one of them in the palm of my hand felt overwhelming.

With my free hand, I reached for the glass of cognac and took a large gulp as if it were some sort of medicine that gave me strength, gumption, and resolution. I put the glass down gingerly on the table beside me and with my other hand I reached for one of her breasts, cupped it in my hand as it still lay beneath her top. It felt wonderful, like a small sponge pillow.

"You probably should not be doing that," she said. I heard her words, but ignored her intention. I kept my hand there. She did nothing except to say I shouldn't be doing that. She didn't pull away, or scream "rape" or immediately get up and tell me to leave. We both sat quietly as I rubbed her breast. If she liked it, she didn't say, but neither did she respond with any moves of her own.

The excitement of the moment urged me on. I attempted to lay her backward onto the couch. My intent was to begin kissing as well as rubbing both breasts. I wasn't sure what kind of contortion of the body this might entail, but the erection and the cognac urged me on. In my haste, I thought a prone position to be more conducive for sexual foreplay.

"We really should *NOT* be doing this," she said. She attempted to get herself up from the couch as she struggled with the weight of my body. I continued to press against her, not in a forceful, aggressive manner, but just enough, I hoped, to give her the impression that I wanted sex with her. By this time, I could not seem to elicit any conversation; I was too intent upon the physical demands. Talk just did not seem necessary.

She gave a mighty heave and released herself from under me and sat bolt upright.

"I appreciate your attention," she said, "but I assumed you knew that I was lesbian. After all, you did pick me up at the Grove. "

I heard her words, but they did not immediately hit home with me. Lesbian, I thought, who cares? Her breasts are just as nice as any straight lady's breasts. In the moment of excitement that had overwhelmed me, I was not attentive to minor word differences. She was female, I was male, and I already had my hands on her breasts, I couldn't understand that this didn't excite her as much as it excited me.

"You need to back off *RIGHT NOW*," she said, emphasizing the right now. I told you I appreciated the attention, but this is not right for me, especially not now."

She had managed to push me away. I obliged and stood the rest of the way myself without her physical urging. I stood there feeling deflated and demoralized. Once again, I felt rejected. Slowly the term "lesbian" began to sink in. What was I thinking? Why didn't I recognize the clues, the short hair, no makeup, hanging out at the Grove. All I could see was a female who took a concerted interest in me late one night who had all the trappings of a lady on the prowl. I felt as if she almost begged me for intimacy.

"I needed to talk to someone halfway intelligent," she began to say, "I had this horrendous fight with my girlfriend while we were at the Grove. I was feeling dejected and lonely, and there you were. I'm sorry if I gave you the wrong impression, but you do understand, don't you?" She had a soulful look on her face as if she had just admitted to a lie for which she was now feeling guilty.

"I was married once, for a short time," she told me, "but it wasn't long before I realized who I really was. I can't go back now."

By this time, both as a result of the booze and, I suspect, of the sudden realization that my intentions of getting lucky had vanished completely, my erection sagged in my pants. It was a truly awkward moment, very embarrassing.

"Why did you let me get this far before you told me that," I said.

"You were kind to me. You helped me up the stairs, got me home safely. I felt obliged."

"Well, I hope you work things out with your friend," I told her.

She offered me another drink as if apologizing for her mistreatment, but I refused. I left without another word. I stumbled down her deck steps and got into my cab. No damage done, I figured, no criminal acts committed, nothing happened to which I needed to feel guilty or ashamed, but nevertheless, I felt devastated. Embarrassed was an understatement; mortified was a better choice.

I drove toward Water Island, as it was too late for working the taxi routes. When I reached home, I had another beer or two and got into bed. Sleep eluded me. My mind continued to rehash the night's events. I felt ashamed and personally embarrassed that, even after so much time in the company of gays and lesbians, I still couldn't distinguish them from straight people. Three years I had waited for this moment, dreamed about it, fantasized, and in an instant, it all vanished. The ideal summer job just never seemed to materialize. How would I explain to my friends, if I ever would, that I had the hots for a lesbian and lost?

17

Queer Culture

*Cherry Grove is the epicenter of High Camp and
Outré fashion.*

--Anonymous

Between Fire Island Pines and Cherry Grove, a small red
flag waved briskly in a light breeze. It stood alone on top of
a remote sand dune. For years, this flag had withstood the
weather, wind, and waves, beckoning those who knew of
its existence to come hither. Like a beacon to the wayfarer,
it marked the precise location toward which many travelers
were drawn.

No houses rimmed the nearby dunes. Few people walked
the beach. The restaurants and pavilions one might associate
with a beach resort were noticeably absent. Occasionally a
lone seagull alighted atop the pole that held the small red
flag. The place looked isolated. Scrub oak and beach plum
bushes dotted the top of the barren rolling sand dune. Yet,
this flag marked a celebrated location visited by a sizable
population at all hours of the day and night.

It was shortly after three o'clock on a Friday afternoon
in July. I sat alone in my taxi at Fire Island Pines. A single
man approached and requested I take him to Cherry Grove,
about two miles further down the beach. I agreed, he got
in, and together we headed west out of the Pines. When

about halfway to the Grove, my passenger suddenly leaned forward and spoke barely above a whisper.

"Tell you what. Drop me off at the meat rack,"

"Excuse me?" I responded. "What did you say?"

"Up there, drop me off by the flag on the dunes."

I knew precisely what he meant. I had made this trip dozens of times, knew where he was headed, but felt I needed to sound naïve and unpretentious. I slowed the taxi down, drove up close to the base of the dunes, and stopped just below the flag. He handed me the three dollar taxi charge and exited. He offered no tip. We exchanged no words. My suspicions were that he had been here many times previously.

I watched him as he scrambled to the top of the dunes. He looked around cautiously as if consumed by humiliation. He ascended over the dune and disappeared from my sight. I thought him too purposeful to be embarrassed. I suspected he fully intended to come to this place; it wasn't a spur of the moment second thought. I didn't think it was a clandestine affair. My intuition was that he had an urge to "hook up" with someone, perhaps even a stranger. Rarely did I ever sense that patrons of the meat rack made prearranged appointments with someone in particular.

I was about to drive away when I detected two men coming back down the same path. They waved at me with a gesture that implied, "Wait a minute, we're coming with you." I waited. They got in my cab and told me they wished to return to the Pines. Neither of the two uttered a word the entire trip. The expectation during the trip to the meat rack was conversations be kept to a minimum. Cab drivers, to avoid sordid details, didn't ask unnecessary questions.

The little flag on the dunes marked the "official" entrance to the meat rack. During all the years I drove a taxi on Fire Island, and I suspect many years before, the meat rack existed. It wasn't listed on tourist maps nor in any of the "things to do" brochures. Everybody knew it was there, but no one acknowledged openly its presence or purpose. The meat rack was less a definitive place but rather an environs, a vicinity toward which gay men gravitated. It had no defined borders and no opening or closing hours; it was available 24/7. In recent years, the destination took on more alluring names such as "the Enchanted Forest," "the Bridge of Sighs," or "The Judy Garland Memorial Park," but its function remained fundamental. I had a vague idea, actually a very clear perception, of its purpose and how it got its name but felt no need to expound. Left to one's imagination, the mere name "meat rack" conjured up its own inventive interpretations.

Fire Island has been a mecca for gay people, particularly men, for decades. Much of its notorious myth revolves around one community in particular--Cherry Grove. The other gay community, Fire Island Pines, was established considerably later.

The "Grove" first emerged as a destination on Fire Island about 1869 when a Long Island entrepreneur began serving seafood dinners to visitors who sailed across the bay for a holiday on the beach. Later, this same industrious man was encouraged to open a hotel with a few adjoining cottages for those wishing to spend the night.

During the 1920's word spread that artists, writers, and theater people from New York and other Broadway elite inhabited (or co-inhabited) the Grove during summer retreats. Numerous sources from that time implied that to be a "theatre person" was synonymous with being gay, although none in the profession openly affirmed this assertion. Neither did they deny it. It was the "in" place to be if you were a writer, editor, poet, movie star, or male model. It has been reported that Oscar Wilde, whose sexual identity has been variously labeled as bisexual, homosexual, and/ or pederastic (likes young boys) frequented Cherry Grove and declared it as "one of the most beautiful resorts" he had witnessed. One can't be sure if he referred to the habitat or the personnel.

Convention maintained that the unincorporated hamlet was named for a grove of cherry trees that once flourished in that location. When my grandparents owned a home there, before the 1938 hurricane and prior to the influx of gay people, cherry trees were still evident. The great hurricane of 1938 destroyed the last remaining trees along with my grandparents' home.

Despite living in the liberal bastion of New York City, being gay prior to the 1980's was an exercise in primordial survival. Except in Greenwich Village, where bohemian bars and clubs flourished and gays congregated, the general public considered homosexuality as deviant behavior and it was overtly condemned. Gay people ran the risk of social ostracism, not to mention loss of business, denial of rental contracts, and the labeling as "perverted."

New York newspapers reveled in stories of raids upon known homosexual hangouts. Despite constant complaints of harassment and prejudice, police protection for gays was virtually non-existent. Unlike African Americans who couldn't hide their skin color, gays did have the option of hiding their sexuality. It was the practice of most gays to remain deeply closeted for protection and sanity.

Fire Island was one place where the gay community could feel at home while not being too far from home. Here they could exhibit their homosexuality away from the ostracism and harassment of public indignation. At Cherry Grove, gays were in abundance, the majority. As one writer stated, "Cherry Grove became the name uttered in secret among gay men and lesbians as a place where they could be as outrageous as they wanted, outside the prying eyes of the general public" ("Is The Grove Getting Its Groove Back?" by Steve Weinstein, *New York Blade,* July, 2004).

By the 1960's, both Cherry Grove and the newer community of Fire Island Pines had found their groove. They defined Fire Island as a gay resort and a top-ten destination for the homosexual community. Their reputations spread far and wide. Commenting in the *New York Times Weekender Magazine* (July 15, 2005), Beth Greenfield describes the gay community of Cherry Grove and Fire Island Pines as "a wonderful environment where you could be gay and open and hold hands and enjoy life…it was a phenomenal place."

AIDS had not yet been discovered in the late 50's and 60's, at least not with any urgency or fear among the gay residents of Fire Island. The reality of sexually transmitted diseases had been around for centuries but was no more associated with homosexuals than with heterosexuals. There was a particular sociological phenomenon occurring among the gay community on Fire Island peculiar to the times. The gay population of Fire Island maintained a benign disinterest in things medical or political relating to the health and welfare of being gay. The early 60's was before the Stonewall gay resistance movement and the emerging Gay Pride revolutions that evolved during the 70's and 80's. The whole point of coming to Fire Island was to escape from the critical and probing scrutiny of the public's general intimidation and simply act as gay as one pleased. To do so with the fear of catching some dread disease was to defeat the point of being present on Fire Island.

The gay status of Fire Island became nationally notorious. I once traveled through North Dakota and spent a night in a small motel in the middle of the state. I chanced to engage the owner in conversation, reminiscing about places we liked hanging out on hot afternoons in summer. I mentioned my love for Fire Island and was about to expound its many virtues when suddenly I was interrupted.

"Isn't that where all the queers flock?" the owner asked. "I think I read about that in the *New York Times.*"

"Well not everybody there is gay," I offered. "My family used to have a home there." This last reference seemed to evoke some association in his mind. Rather meekly he said, "You're not gay are you? I mean I have nothing against homo's. I was just wondering."

The phrase, "I have nothing against homo's" felt surprisingly similar to those who claim to "have many friends who are Black." It's a revelation of one's blatant attitudes of bias. He pretended to be curious and innocent, but I suspected him of being judgmental. Probably an equally judgmental attitude on my part

"I think I hear my wife calling," I told him. I excused myself and left.

Most psychologists classified homosexuality as a pathological disease until 1973. Homophobia, the prejudicial fear and loathing of homosexuals and the mindset that is partially to blame for keeping homosexuality as a "perversion," became a catch-phrase in the middle of the 60's. Homophobes intensified contempt and reinforced prejudice toward gays. As I remember, the characterization of gays portrayed in the media, especially by comics who mimicked, in exaggerated form, supposed homosexual effeminate attributes influenced my attitudes. I thought these hyperboles clever and funny and probably accurate.

Growing up, I was as much in the fog about queer culture as the rest of America. Elementary school textbooks and health education classes mentioned nothing about homosexuality. I did learn about *Homo sapiens,* however, and offered my own inferences. In my innocence, I thought Homosexuals were *Homo sapiens* who married and had children (called procreation). My sex education was extremely undistinguished.

In junior high, during recess, I learned differently. I became homophobic and mastered the terminology and techniques. If some kid in school acted weird--didn't roll his tee shirt sleeves up properly, didn't like to make out at parties, or thought the music of Elvis Presley was demonic— we labeled him queer.

"Man, are you gay or what? What are you, a fag?"

If he talked about anything other than sports or girls, he was a fairy. If he liked reading or played the piano or joined the cooking club, he was a smurf. Name-calling was intentional, a means meant to bully, to intimidate, to accentuate the superiority of the name-caller. And was it ever effective and menacing. Calling someone else "queer" was highly incendiary; it reinforced one's own masculinity.

Growing up on Fire Island, Cherry Grove was always off limits. In our isolated community of Water Island we suspected a few residents to be gay playwrights; the prevailing attitude, however, remained one of cautious tolerance or complete denial.

"It's a homo haven," my father reminded us whenever we asked if we could hike down the beach to Cherry Grove. "It's no place for you kids to be hanging out." We reminded him that his family once had a house there. They might still be there if the hurricane of '38 had not washed it away

"That was before the homo's moved in." End of conversation.

My cousin Harvey got a real nice Lyman lap streak sided outboard motor boat one summer. Together we spent many days water skiing on the bay and traveling to different communities at the east end of the Island – Davis Park, Watch Hill, Long Cove, and even as far as the Moriches Inlet. Going west was another story.

We planned a day trip one time down west to the Sunken Forest, a unique area of low lying swamp, bunched beach grass, and oak trees entangled with vines. It was a haven for the small deer and fox that populated the Island. In those days it remained wild and barely visited.

"That's too close to Cherry Grove," Uncle Harvey told us. "There's liable to be some queers walking around." These words uttered from a man who made his livelihood by selling groceries and beach supplies to Fire Island residents. I think he confused the Sunken Forest with the meat rack, then known by the name of the Enchanted Forest.

Later, as a White Cap driver, I had numerous occasions to wander through the myriad of boardwalks that ramble through Cherry Grove. It never failed to intrigue me. I imagined the feeling of Alice upon entering the Land of Oz. It was like being in a wonderland. Fashion was outré, architecture quirky, music saucy, and beach attire brief but not quite bare.

The interior and exterior decoration of cottages was particularly eclectic. Homes ranged from typical A-frames to huge double-floored wonders in the style of Venetian palazzos. "Some houses are simple and ramshackle, fronted by small, sandy yards or beach grass and collections of colorful bouys, while others are grand, surrounded by high wire fences and clutches of bamboo and elaborate gardens." (Beth Greenfield, New York Times, July 15. 2005). Notwithstanding the size, each seemed styled with a meticulous sense of design, some elaborately conceived with towers, multi-layered decks, statues, antique fountains, and Corinthian columns. House colors were not the usual brown-shingled variety one might expect of summer beach cottages. Pastels were prominent – pink, mauve, chartreuse, cyan, or magenta. Residents christened their cottages with names the way children are often baptized - the Liberty Bell, Belvedere, the Funk House, Upson Downs, Seastheday, Xanadu, Terrapinstation, Beau-He-Man-Rhapsody, and Openyourheart. Often the names reflected the personality or disposition of the owners. Regardless of size, residents took great pride and creativity in landscaping with painstakingly intricate English gardens, potted plants, and miniature roses, most of which were not native and had to be custom imported and designed. One house had a miniature railroad layout encircling the front garden.

Cherry Grove was a safe place. Despite being predominately gay, there existed no feeling of exclusiveness. No "gays only" signs existed, innuendos that straight people were not welcomed. It amazed me that those in the gay community could be so welcoming of straight people after the intimidation they endured in the straight community. If I felt any uneasiness, it was due to the feeling of being lured into a fantasy world where most of the people were better looking, better educated, and had a greater self-esteem than anything I could muster up for myself. Yes, I felt envious at times and wondered often what it would be like to be gay. Would I acquire some of the same talents displayed by so many in the gay community? Even though I had no inner feelings of becoming gay--I could not comprehend the idea of a man with another man sexually--acceptance of the life-style became easier the longer I stayed on the Island.

Gays were the majority population at Cherry Grove and Fire Island Pines. They set the standards. They created the expectations. Their social attitudes and behaviors were the norm rather than the exception. The attitude of acceptance served as a safety valve that allowed the residents freedom to blow off steam and to temporarily escape from the pressure of being closeted. It was their chosen place to act outrageously gay without commitment or consequences.

Cruising without obligation was not only accepted, it was encouraged. The meat rack served a purpose.

Parties abounded. Invitations seemed unnecessary. As I walked among the closely clustered houses on the boardwalks of Cherry Grove after 9:00 in the evening on days off or even on days on, it seemed every other house emanated with music and laughter. If I happened to stop and stare and someone noticed, an invitation to "come on in" was forthcoming. No need to ask my name. I was included despite attired only in jeans and a tee shirt and most of the group assembled wore pastel colored ruffled shirts open down the front and string bikinis or short shorts that left little to the imagination

"Want something to drink?" They asked me immediately. Before I could respond, they handed me something pink and fluffy in a fluted glass.

"Thanks," I said. "What is this?"

"My own concoction. And you'll love it, honey." It seemed everyone's name was "honey."

On days off, I would use the jeep to cruise around looking for hot spots of action--Cherry Grove or the Pines--always hoping to find some excitement where I would feel comfortable and included. Being shy and reserved by nature, I was never confident that I would recognize action, if it did happen to materialize. My persistent inhibition was my nemesis. I lacked assertiveness, and harbored feelings of inadequacy. I also felt a bit squeamish around gay people after so many years under the influence of homophobes.

Robert, a twenty-something aspiring model who frequented my cab, kept asking me to join him at the Shack, one of the more popular bars at Cherry Grove. I felt comfortable with Robert. He didn't seem consumed by his gayness. He and I had some interests in common--photography, college, and marriage, but to differing genders. He claimed his friends would like me and his challenge aroused my sense of adventure.

I parked the taxi on the beach at the foot of the stairs leading up to the Shack. On weekends, the Shack was full of "guests," straight people from other communities we taxied down to the Grove to ogle at the queer culture. On weeknights, however, mostly gay men patronized it. I could hear Edith Piaf, in her soulful French accent, playing on the jukebox. I went in. The place was full of guys; hardly a female was in sight. I had become skilled at identifying gays; something about their demeanor, their fashion, their walk. Robert was leaning on the bar, deeply engaged in conversation with two other guys. He noticed me standing in the doorway and approached me.

"You look like you're scared to death to be here," he said.

"Why do you say that?" I continued searching the room with my eyes.

"You've got that frightened glow about you, as if you suspect any minute someone's gonna grab you by the balls. You're safe here. Relax."

Robert introduced me to his friends, telling them I was straight and I drove one of the beach taxis. "But don't hold that against him," he added. "He's really a dear, just a bit apprehensive about being around gays." It sounded like he was offering an apology on my behalf for being straight. I smiled, feeling self-conscious, almost wishing that what he said wasn't true. I felt vulnerable and defenseless, out of my element and under great scrutiny by suspicious eyes. The room reeked of Canoe cologne. The perfumed air only added to my discomfort.

"Being a straight guy must be hard for you, hard for anyone," one of Robert's friends said. "But we aren't chauvinists."

"Robert's a dear," his friend Timothy piped in. "If we got to love him then we got to love you. Robert is letting us stay with him a few days"

In the company of these three, I thought I would feel as if being straight was a liability. Robert, Timothy, and the third friend seemed in a talkative mood. They put me at ease with their ready acceptance and feeling of inclusion. I took this as an invitation to express my curiosity.

"You're living here with Robert?" I said. "What do you like about the Grove?"

"It's gay, famously gay," Timothy responded. "It's so refreshing to be able to act gay, be gay without a hassle. Even in the city, you have to swallow your self-respect or you take your life in your hands if you want to be openly gay. Here I can be as gay as I want. Everybody's gay here, well almost." He looked at me apologetically. "It's so emptying," he said.

"What do you mean, emptying?" I asked him.

"Like emptying. Like when you suddenly realize that all that garbage you've been stashing in the cellar to keep it out of sight is beginning to stink up the whole house so you get rid of it all and the house begins to smell sweeter and cleaner. When I am here, I don't have to hide my shit. I don't stink."

Living in a gay community proved to be an epiphany for me. I became ambivalent, vacillating between a nagging infatuation with gay culture and an inner repulsion of gay sexuality. I wondered why homosexuality was so maligned. I began to realize that sexuality was a small portion of one's personality and character; it didn't reveal the whole person. I became fascinated by and somewhat in awe of the accomplishments of the gay community. Gays far outweighed the general population in what they contributed to society--music, art, theatre, literature. What the homosexual population has achieved, they have had to do under adverse conditions, always with undertones of being perverse and in an atmosphere of having to hide a part of their identity. For the summer, however, I was a visitor in their community, subject to their culture, exposed to their norms and, as such, expected to abide by their expectations. The sensation of being welcomed unconditionally always felt a bit suspicious to me, having been brought up in a conservative New England prep school where each person had to prove himself before being accepted, but the change was refreshing.

Straight people chose to visit these communities for the expressed purpose of joining in this culture, at least on a temporary basis. More than curiosity motivated them. Their intent seemed always one of seeking out the good time that the gay community created and hosted, to feast on the cuisine that was notorious for being balsamic, dulcet, nectarous, and gustatory and always on the scrumptious and succulent side of the taste buds, to gawk at the antics, observe the costumes, and then join in the party atmosphere that gay men conjured so easily. No expectations in the queer culture: you are who you are.

My summers spent living in, but not of, the gay community proved to be an epiphany. I became, at the very least, ambivalent, vacillating between a nagging infatuation of gay culture and an inner repulsion of gay sexuality. Daily contact with gays provided perceptions about homosexuality I never wondered about previously. I had to confront directly my own phobias. I wondered if I loathed homosexual sexuality because I feared I might have the same tendencies myself.

It was a bit of an exaggeration to classify all gays on Fire Island as outrageous; ostentatious perhaps, a bit flamboyant or bordering on the obnoxious, but clearly not totally outrageous. I figured that because gays constituted the majority at Cherry Grove and Fire Island Pines, they were entitled to dictate the life-style.

18

The Taxi Rodeo

Calling a taxi on Fire Island is like calling a robber in Iraq.

--Anonymous

In parts of the city where nightlife is pulsing, competition for a cab can get fiercer than a fashion show runway; angling for a ride home turns into a contact sport for drivers and riders.

--CBSlocal.com, May 15,2012

I have a driver's license, but the truth is that I hardly ever drive. I prefer to get around by taxi.

--Ferran Adria

Riding in a beach taxi is not considered a contact sport. You expect it not to be perilous. Safety, however, was never the highest priority for the drivers. This was a summer job. There was a very short window for making some money; perhaps three months or a bit longer and then it was all over for the year. For me, profit took precedence over all other considerations except perhaps impressing the ladies. I never purposefully intended for anyone to get hurt while riding in my taxi, but I was always mindful that the more passengers at any one time, the greater the profit. I was at least aware, if not fully attentive, that crowded conditions meant greater risk. Drivers disregarded the welfare and security of the passengers, however, in favor of other objectives. Show me the money.

The taxis themselves did not have a reputation as being dependable and secure. They were old and dilapidated. Years of use and abuse had taken their toll. First manufactured in the 1950's, these vehicles had a similar design to the World War II jeeps. These jeeps functioned under extreme duress: in off-road terrain, under harsh conditions, and by drivers who could not care about maintenance. They were rugged and not particularly comfortable. Following the conclusion of the war, when the open-topped, two-seated army-style jeep was no longer needed, the Willys Company converted the design into a four-seater, put a top on the vehicle, and fashioned it to resemble a box of wheels. The company retained the four-wheeled drive mechanism until the mid-1960's when the more modern jeep replaced it produced by the Chrysler Corporation and sold as the precursor to the SUV.

By hook or by crook, Roger and Everett rounded up a number of these old Willys jeeps still in running condition and, if not already painted red, repainted them red and capped them off with a white top and a little dome light on the roof just to make them look like authentic taxis. Then they hauled them across the bay on barges or drove them over the Smith Point Bridge during the winter months.

Both Everett and Roger were inventive mechanics. They each possessed an instinct for diagnosing auto mechanical problems and on the spot, instant jerry-rigged maintenance. With a little bailing wire, some duct tape, a section of garden hose, a can of WD40, and an assortment of nuts and bolts, they could instantly fix whatever might be ailing an indisposed jeep. I marveled at their innovation and abilities.

One of the unique characteristics of the Willys Jeep, and a boon to the taxi business, was the fold-down back tailgate. When opened, it laid down flat like a truck tailgate, only larger. The upper portion, with an attached inset window, could also be raised, thus leaving a large cave-like opening in the rear of the boxy body, big enough into which a refrigerator could be coaxed. This large opening was an invitation to the drivers; better yet a challenge, to see how they could accommodate additional passengers, comfortably, or uncomfortably. Money talks, and more passengers meant increased profits.

The open tailgate also served as an enticement for adventurous passengers. They loved to sit back there. What better way to experience a summer evening then a moon-light ride along a beautiful beach with the soft sound of waves breaking and salt air filling the lungs while dragging one's bare feet in the wet sand? That gas fumes billowed up and into the rear compartment was of little consequence. This sort of venture could only be done while riding on the tailgate. For the truly romantic, the thought was irresistible. Passengers often requested to be seated back there rather than inside the cab, even when room inside was available.

"Can we sit on the tailgate?" was a constant question, even when the cab was empty.

"If you want," I would reply. "But don't let your feet dangle over the back. Could get caught on some driftwood and bang you up pretty bad." I usually cautioned riders, but in fact, I actually could not have cared less. That was the thrill of riding on the tailgate: letting your feet dangle and occasionally getting them wet while we drove through the remnants of a tide pool. The passenger's safety was a non-issue. If they were oblivious to the risks, so was I.

"Oh . . . This is so much fun." I heard from the back of the taxi, along with much giggling.

No one complained. Riding on the tailgate of a taxi was the epitome of beach transportation. If the person was dressed in something other than normal beach attire – a sun dress, pants and a sweater, a white dinner jacket – they were welcome to ride inside the cab. Few requests were forth-coming despite the more formal dress. The insides of the taxis were not noted for being exceptionally clean, not even close. It was always a crap-shoot to ride anywhere in or about the cab when one wanted to look presentable when leaving the cab.

The tailgate invited a language all its own. As people eyed the open area in the rear, it elicited comments such as,

"You can get a suntan back here," or "The best view of the ocean is from the back," or "I like to see where I've been and not worry about where I'm going." Most of the time, the experience just provoked giggles and hilarity with only a slight chance for disaster. The tailgate was the preferred seat in the taxi despite any warning I might give to the contrary.

Efficiency, comfort, and convenience were not a priority when choosing a taxi. It was the adventure, the escapade, which often prodded riders. The taxi ride was an integral part of whatever experience they planned. The journey seemed as important as the destination. It was entertainment, like a Disney World ride, not just another obstacle in the way of getting somewhere. The "piling in" of as many people as possible in the open space of the tailgate, especially when all were in a jovial party mood, was not an annoyance to customers, but rather an anticipated delight. Being slightly inebriated only enhanced the experience.

From over the radio, I heard Paul, our taxi dispatcher, announce a potential fare and request a response. "Party of seven wants to go to the Grove. Who's got it?" It was a weekday evening with few potential fares. At the moment, most of the other drivers were out of their cabs eating at the restaurant in Fire Island Pines.

"I got it," I responded immediately. "Where are they?"

They're at Beach Walkway at Ocean Bay Park. Want an eight o'clock pickup."

"Got it," I reiterated.

"Ten-four," Paul responded, the official radio phrase signaling acknowledgment.

At 8:00 I sat in my taxi at Beach Walkway. No one was waiting. Having little patience, I was just about to leave when a woman appeared at the top of the steps leading down to the beach. She spotted me and began waving her arms frantically. I could hear her calling to people behind her, "He's here." She descended the steps, but when nearing the bottom, she fell face first into the soft sand. She immediately picked herself up before I could assist her, brushed the sand off her print sun dress, and said, "I'm okay. No problem." She giggled while she spoke. "The others are coming right along." She didn't appear embarrassed by her mishap. It was as if she choreographed the whole episode. Then I smelled her breath and understood the reason for the tumble.

She wore a pullover beach dress, the kind people slipped over their heads while still wearing a bathing suit. She had her shoes in her hands, pink sandals, having taken them off after her spill down the stairs. She carried no purse and wore no jewelry. She stood by the side of the taxi, adjusting her dress and brushing her windblown hair away from her face. She started a conversation telling me how she liked the feel of the cool sand between her toes.

"That's nice," I told her. "When are the others coming?"

I listened to the chatter on the radio, which had picked up since other drivers had returned from eating supper. New calls were beginning to come through, some only a few boardwalks down from where I parked. I'm thinking, "If these others are not here in a few minutes, I'm leaving this lady on the beach with shoes on or not. I'll tell her I'll be back in thirty minutes, maybe." She sensed my frustration.

"Can you wait just a minute?" she told me. "I'll go and see what's keeping them."

"Okay," I agreed. "But I'll need to move on soon cause we got others waiting." It was a lie, but the threat usually worked.

She struggled up the staircase and disappeared over the top of the stairway.

I learned that people who reserve a taxi are rarely on time. They think that because they called for a cab, they owned it. People on vacation had a very different concept of time, or better yet, no concept of time. They choose to come to the island so they could relax, sleep late, and take their sweet time with whatever plans they made. It irritated the hell out of me, but I understood the mindset. Observing time constraints meant nothing until late Sunday afternoon when they had to catch the last ferry leaving the island. Then, even when we were on time, customers criticized us for lingering too long or not driving fast enough.

Soon my fare was back. She hurried down the stairs, this time without tumbling. "They're on their way," she told me.

She sounded out of breath.

I heard laughing and singing coming from a group of people as they looked down the staircase toward the beach and my taxi parked below. Seven people, all adults, began to descend the stairs. They held on to each other for balance. They all seemed to have trouble negotiating the steps. Some carried drink glasses with something pink and foamy inside which spilled a little at each step. It didn't take a genius to surmise I had a party of drunks. Being drunk is not a moral transgression nor against any regulations for riding in a cab, unless you are the driver. Even then, it's tolerated, as few cared and no one checked.

The group surrounded the cab, as if trying to figure out where the doors were located and how to get in. The giggling continued. Conversations were in tandem, all of which I failed to comprehend. One in the group discovered the tailgate closed except for the top portion.

"Let's ride back here," I heard from a muddled voice. "Hey cabbie, can we ride on the tailgate?"

I started toward the back. "What the hell," I figured. "Can't do much harm. And they are too drunk to convince otherwise."

"We'll be real careful," they assured me. "It'll be groovy back here. Please." A group of inebriants can carry on *ad infinitum* without wearing down. It was useless to resist their insistence.

Some had already gotten themselves onto the tailgate and began contorting their bodies into various shapes in order to make room for others. I asked that they please not dangle their feet over the side. I rehearsed the dangers, but my admonitions fell on deaf ears as the tailgate became so crowded that some feet had no place else to go, but over the edge. All seven managed to squeeze into the rear of the cab with three or four sitting directly on the tailgate.

The jeep had a noticeable slump in the rear as the weight of seven people was concentrated there. I eased myself into the driver's seat. It felt like I was looking slightly uphill. I started the engine and slowly began to drive toward the

Grove. I heard laughing and jabbering and felt bouncing in the far back of the cab, all signs they were enjoying the ride or just acting drunk. I proceeded with caution; I wanted to avoid any mishaps.

I occasionally checked my rear view mirror. My thoughts were that taxi insurance companies must have rules forbidding riding on the tailgate, despite that all drivers allowed it. I didn't remember any question regarding tailgate etiquette on my chauffeur's driver license test. I was sure it was against all regulations for driving on roads in the State of New York. But this was Fire Island, and there were no roads. I let out a relaxed sigh and kept driving.

I noticed the tide receding quickly, leaving a hard surface down by the water's edge. I headed toward the surf and shifted into a higher gear. The jeep responded with increased speed. I watched the early moon cast its light on the curling waves. It sparkled as it reflected off the constantly moving water.

It was dusk. Suddenly I noticed something large caught in the beam of my headlights. It looked like driftwood left behind by the outgoing tide. I swerved sharply to one side to avoid hitting it, but felt the back tire bounce over the log. There was a substantial jounce but nothing drastic. We leveled off and continued on our way.

From the back of the cab, the laughter became more boisterous. I smiled as I thought, "they must be enjoying the ride." Then, through the din of noises I heard, "Wait. Stop. Stop the taxi." There was more yelling and more laughter. Something was wrong. I brought the cab to an immediate halt.

Amidst the talking and laughter, I heard, "We lost Albert."

I got out and walked to the rear. Two of the people already stood in the sand.

"When we hit that bump, we lost Albert," one of them told me. The two who were standing in the sand began walking back towards where we had come.

"You mean he fell out of the cab?"

"Yes, he's back there somewhere."

"Get back in the cab," I told the rest who were now all standing in the sand. "We'll go back and look for him."

I turned the taxi around, and we headed back down the beach. Within a few hundred yards my headlights glimpsed Albert sitting in the sand while waves washed around his feet. The two walkers caught up to us. Everyone exited the cab and we stood around Albert. Albert looked dazed, confused, but unharmed.

"You okay, Albert?" asked everyone at the same time. There was much chatter and jabber as they poked and probed Albert in an attempt to decipher if any bruises existed.

"You were there one second and gone the next," one of the group exclaimed followed by hilarious laughter.

"That was an excellent half-gainer, you did," another person said. More laughter followed.

No one seemed overly concerned about Albert's physical condition. I asked directly, "Are you hurting anywhere? Does anything feel broken?"

"Not that I can tell," Albert replied.

He got up slowly from his sitting position, and his friends brushed the sand from his wet clothes with great difficulty. Albert's clothes appeared to cause him some stress.

"Shit," Albert blurted out. "My new pants are full of wet sand and it's in my underwear. If I scratch my ass, I'll probably peel my skin off. And I lost one of my sandals."

After some more scrutinizing of his body parts by his friends, they declared Albert healthy. Except for his clothes, he was certainly not upset or angered by his fall. He was still having a good time.

I suggested that Albert ride inside for the remainder of the trip. The resounding "no" that came from the group sounded like a chorus. Albert didn't protest. Instead, he climbed back onto the tailgate.

"We're having too much fun back here," they all agreed. "Albert's fine. I got my arms wrapped around him and I'm holding him by his balls."

We got to the Grove without further mishap. They all piled out of the rear of the taxi while I counted heads just to make sure I hadn't lost someone. Albert appeared just fine, minus one sandal.

"That was the most fun," I heard one person say as I collected my fare. In addition to the fare, one in the group handed me a five-dollar bill. "This is for you," she said. "That ride was far out. Really enjoyed it. We need to do this again soon."

I reminded her that she'll have to get back to Ocean Bay Park later that evening, unless she wanted to stay at the Grove.

"We'll look forward to it, sweetie," she told me. They disappeared up the steps in front of Pat's Place.

I worried that Albert might have gotten hurt but wouldn't realize it until the next day. Then he would want to sue the pants off White Cap Taxi. I debated telling Roger what happened. Should I prepare him just in case? I decided against revealing anything and took my chances that Albert wasn't hurt or, better yet, won't remember.

Six hours later, at two-thirty in the morning, three taxis lined up in front of Pat's Place. Terry was first in line. I saw Albert and company descending the stairs, stumbling as they negotiated each step. They headed for the first taxi and surrounded Terry's cab. I then heard the chorus of voices. "Can we ride on the tailgate?" All I could think of was "good luck, Terry."

19

Fire on Fire Island

Ctesibius of Alexandria is credited with inventing the first fire pump around the second century B.C. Colonial laws of America required each house to have a bucket of water on the front stoop (especially at night) in case of fire for the initial bucket brigade that would throw the water on the fire.

--Wikipedia

On Fire Island fire was our worst enemy; it was the nemesis of every homeowner. With no professional fire departments, at least not in the smaller villages, and a laid-back attitude about Herculean efforts toward any task during a summer vacation, any fire other than a wienie roast on the beach caused great anxiety among the residents.

The threat of a fire becoming disastrous loomed large. The wind constantly blew. There was no reliable water supply, other than the ocean. Fire departments consisted of beer drinking volunteers. Wood was the primary construction material in all the homes. No homeowner was immune from the potential of a calamitous fire. Once ignited, a house fire would not quit until the building burned to the ground.

Our parents were vigilant about not playing with fire. A favorite pastime growing up was the traditional marshmallow roast by a beachfront campfire. The wind direction determined if beach fires happened. If it blew in from the south toward the land, caution ruled and beach fires were prohibited. We ate raw marshmallows. If the wind blew from the north, out towards the ocean, no problem. Often our marshmallow roasts were merely excuses for making out with girls on the beach. When fear of fire disabled our plans, no problem, we moved the make-out parties to other locations.

Clambakes were an exception. We dug a hole in the sand. We lighted a fire down in the hole and watched vigilantly until it burned down to hot coals. Then we placed the fresh clams in their shells wrapped in damp cloths down into the burning coals. The fire never really burned, it only smoldered. The steam cooked the clams. This was a controlled burn and elicited minimal fear from residents.

Fire Islanders held a fatalistic attitude about fires. On the one hand, they fully respected and feared fires and did all they could to take necessary precautions against unwanted ones. On the other hand, when a fire broke out, they accepted the inevitable; that there was nothing much they could do except watch it burn itself out.

One time while I was staying at my Aunt Ethel's house, I awoke to loud conversation in the adjoining room. It was 3:30 in the morning. Outside the window I could see the night sky lit up like a ball park. I first thought it was the sun beginning to rise but then heard voices talking about a house fire. I jumped out of bed, pounded my cousin Harvey on the head to wake him, and we both hurried into the other room.

"Joe Gerard's house down by the dock is on fire," Aunt Ethel informed us. "Your father has gone down to see if he can help."

"Can we go and see?" we both asked simultaneously.

"I suppose so, but put some shoes on. And stay out of people's way".

My cousin and I always slept in our bathing suits when we were younger. Actually we never changed out of them for any occasion during the summer. If they got wet from swimming, we let them air dry while still on us. By evening, they may have smelled a bit ripe, but no matter. It seemed appropriate to wear them constantly since we were in the water more often than not. We put on our shoes and ran out the door toward the visible flames. When we arrived near the docks, we saw that no one was working to put the flames out; they just stood by talking and watching. No other structures stood nearby and it appeared resignation had set. People merely accepted another house lost. So all watched the house quickly disintegrate as if enjoying a Fourth of July fireworks show. The only thing missing were marshmallows and girls.

"It's a shame," someone watching the fire remarked.

"Wish there was something we could do," another stated.

"I think I remember that Joe just finished painting and fixing up the inside."

"Nothing we can do about it now. Maybe we should have brought some hot dogs." There was a muffled laughter.

We all watched the fire burn the house completely to ground level. Eventually, my cousin and I got bored and went back home to bed. But enough of old remembrances, back to our story.

I had just dropped off a taxi fare at Davis Park and was heading back toward the Pines with the usual empty cab and bemoaning that I had to take the fare at the request of Everett. I vowed to make myself as scarce as possible at Davis Park. To ease my annoyance, I decided to stop off at our house at Water Island before arriving back at the Pines. I was hungry and a baloney sandwich on white bread with gobs of mayonnaise and butter always spiked my spirits. Baloney sandwiches were my salvation that summer. My brother Paul, who was staying at the house, reminded me that I left the mayonnaise out for the last three days and it might be a bit rancid. It made little impression. I took the sandwich with me to the taxi and once again resumed my journey back to the Pines.

Eating and driving at the same time is an art form. It takes creative coordination and considerable dexterity to do this without causing a mess. I was never very good at this skill. Too much mayonnaise made for a very slippery sandwich and I had to keep my eye on both the beach ahead and the oozing mayonnaise at the same time. This one time I looked up and my glance caught sight of some smoke. It was rising from behind the dunes just past the last boardwalk toward the west end of Water Island. It was white, the kind you might expect from a campfire. A new house had just been completed nearby, and I thought the smoke might be from burning the residue of leftover building materials. Often, when the wind was from the north, residents burned their trash rather than carting it off. Residents frowned upon this, but it happened occasionally.

As I approached closer, besides being aware that mayonnaise spilled on my pants, I noticed the smoke plumes were growing in intensity. The color changed from pure white to a light gray. Whatever was burning, it was clearly growing in strength. Curiosity and my inherited trepidation of fires ignited my attention. I needed to check out the source, see if it was under control. Smoke aroused suspicion I couldn't ignore.

I parked the taxi close to the base of the dunes. Ignoring the warning sign – Do Not Walk on Dunes – I climbed to the top. I saw the smoke was coming from the house, but didn't see flames. I couldn't decipher which part of the structure was burning. The smoke obliterated much of the house. I saw no persons attempting to put out the fire.

To the best of my memory, Water Island had never had a house fire. Many decades previous a large hotel had burned down, but that all happened long before the memory of any present homeowners. Our residents association made a yearly plea warning us of the danger of fire, but there was no organized plan in place to combat them with the exception of the construction of a fire gong. A large iron ring, about four feet in diameter (I think it was the remnants of a train engine wheel) had been secured and hung from a wooden frame work near the main public dock. Mounted next to the ring was a large sledge hammer. In case of fire, residents mandated that the gong to be rung several times with the sledge hammer. The noise carried throughout the community. Unfortunately, the hammer kept disappearing.

No particular persons had the assignment to ring the gong and most people assumed that someone else would shoulder the honor. If it rang, there was no predetermined plan of action. For fun, we kids discovered that ringing the gong late at night and then disappearing down the boardwalk tossing the hammer off into the bushes as we ran caused great alarm among the residents. The first few times, a crowd of people showed up with buckets of water. Too many false alarms, however, caused a widespread indifference and suspicion; no one showed up anymore when the gong rang.

One summer, as residents arrived, they noticed a new item meant for fire protection. One resident who owned a mechanical shop had donated a gas powered water pump which he mounted on large wheels and placed adjacent to the fire gong. On its side, he had painted in red letters, "Water Island Pumper No. 1." Attached to its other side was a fifty-foot hose that could connect to the front of the pump. I couldn't vouch that this behemoth had ever been actually field-tested, but it looked ominous and gave the residents an increased sense of security.

As I watched the fire spread, I remembered the fire pump. Always ready for some action, I decided it would be fun, even if not necessary, to solicit its use. There was a fire raging, or so it seemed in my novice estimation, and what other course of action was more appropriate than to make some attempt to put it out. I hadn't yet conceded to the attitude of "let it burn itself out."

I would need some help. My brother Paul was home and always ready for some excitement.

"Well let's go," were his exact words when I got back to the house and described both the fire and my intended course of action. If he were suspicious of my motivations, he didn't show it. Just to be sure, he went outside to have a look and saw the smoke flumes in the distance.

"Let's get the pumper," I said. "We'll pull it along the boardwalk to the beach and then find a way to tie it behind my taxi." He anticipated my very thoughts.

"Let's go," he repeated. "But forget about the gong. No one responds to that anymore."

The pumper weighed a ton, or so it seemed. It proved difficult to drag along the rutted boardwalk. Only our adrenaline kept us going as we trudged from the bay side to the ocean side along the uneven boardwalk, pausing only momentarily to catch our breath and renew our energy. We hesitated at the top of the stairs leading down to the beach front. Our plan was to attach the pumper to the rear of the taxi like a trailer, but first we had to get it down the stairs and onto the beach. Paul and I looked at each other for a moment, said nothing, and then as if symbiotically we both instinctively pushed the pumper down the stairs. It bounced, broke a few of the wooden steps, but miraculously landed right side up.

I attached the pumper to the rear bumper of the taxi with a rope I retrieved from the back of the cab. I started the taxi, but the engine groaned and strained. The clumsy, heavy wheels sunk into the soft sand until we were able to maneuver it closer to the water's edge where the sand remained packed. The pumper then rolled along quite easily behind the jeep.

Smoke continued to billow from behind the dunes, even more so than before. Our next challenge was to get the pumper over the dunes and down toward the house. While Paul stood on top of the dunes surveying the landscape, I maneuvered the taxi and pumper down to the hard sand surface close to the surf. I gave the taxi full throttle and roared straight toward where Paul was pointing at the top of the dunes. Paul continually waved his arms in the air, indicating I should go a little to the left or more to the right as I sped up the side of the dunes.

"The hell with the regulations about dune destruction," I thought. "This must count as an emergency." Better to ask forgiveness than permission under these circumstances, I thought to myself.

Just as I crested the top, Paul jumped clear of the taxi and I careened the jeep on down the other side, stopping only for a moment to allow Paul to catch up and get back in the taxi. Together, we bushwhacked our way across low grass, beach plum bushes, and scrub oak trees toward the still-burning house, all the while the pumper bumped along like a kid in an inner tube towed behind a speeding boat in rough water.

We saw no people and assumed the house was empty. The fire had already consumed the roof, which had collapsed. The fire showed no signs of moderating. Discarded building materials--pieces of cut lumber, insulation, and wooden shingles--lay abandoned beside the house, but not yet consumed by the fire.

"If the trash catches fire," I told Paul, "it could easily spread to the dry bushes and then we got a forest fire."

"Pull the pumper as close to the bay as possible," Paul said. "The short end of the hose has to be in the water. When we get it going, you watch that the hose stays in the water and I'll spray the house with the longer hose." Prior to this, we had made no coordinated plans on how the two of us would play at being firemen. Paul's admonitions sounded practical and workable.

I began to untangle the hoses from off the side of the pumper. The short one was easy but the longer one looked to be at least fifty-feet in length, enough to reach from the pumper placed near the water supply up to the house, but not much further. Paul, on his own initiative, tried starting the gas engine on the pumper. Paul's talents ran deep when it came to starting gasoline engines, and he had the pumper running almost immediately. He left it running and came to my assistance. I was still attempting to untangle the mess of hoses. With pinched fingers and bruised hands, we managed to connect all the pieces together until the hoses lay ready for action. The short one went from the water source in the bay to the pumper. The longer one, under pressure from the pump, was intended to spray the house.

"I'll stay down here by the water and keep this end in the bay," I yelled at Paul. "You're the fireman up at the house." With that, I stuck my end of the hose in the shallow water at the edge of the bay. "Give it some gas now," I said, figuring that with a little humph from the pumper, the water would come blasting out at Paul's end.

Nothing happened. No water.

"What's the matter?" I yelled to Paul.

"No water's coming," He dropped the hose, walked back along its length, and checked for any kinks in the hose. No kinks.

"My end is in the water," I told him. I could plainly see that the suction end was beneath the surface of the bay water. "But wait a minute." I bent over and closely examined the submerged end of the hose. I reached with my hand and felt the end of the nozzle. A large mass of seaweed was stuck tight against the inlet. With both hands, I tugged on the wad until I freed the hose opening of all obstructions. Immediately water gushed forth at Paul's end in a great deluge. Paul reeled back as water shot from the hose, bucking and swinging in all directions. Composing himself, he aimed it at the core of the fire, and just as immediately as it burst forth it slowed to a trickle again.

"What now?" he said disgustedly as he held the limp hose in his hands. "See if it's clogged again."

It was. I pulled more seaweed away from the nozzle and just as quickly it sucked up more water. For the next fifteen minutes my only task was to constantly pull seaweed from the suction end while intermittently Paul doused the fire.

Then the engine stopped. It sputtered a few times and then quit altogether. Paul gave the starter cord great heaves, but nothing happened except to form beads of sweat running down his face.

"It's gotta be out of gas," he said. "Do we have any more gas?"

"No." I thought for a moment. "But maybe I got a solution." Brilliance doesn't become me, but I felt proud that I thought of a solution. I had a short section of garden hose tucked away in the taxi to siphon water from a faucet into my radiator as needed. It was a better solution than having to carry the water from the faucet to the taxi. Laziness is the mother of invention. I also had an empty five-gallon gas can.

Why it was empty, I forgot, but it was.

"This is gonna taste like shit," I told Paul as I began to siphon gas from the taxi fuel tank into the five gallon can. I had to suck on the end of the hose to get the siphon started. As soon as I sensed the slightest taste of gas in my mouth, I directed my end of the hose into the can. I filled the can and poured it into the pumper gas tank.

Paul once again pulled mightily on the starter cord, and soon the pumper engine let out a roar.

"We're back in business," Paul said. Working together, my keeping the suction hose end clear of seaweed and Paul keeping the business end of the hose pointed at the fire, it was only a matter of a few minutes until we saw that the flames all but disappear. Only smoldering ambers remained.

Only when the fire was under control did other people begin to show their faces. Some brought shovels and heaped sand on the ashes, the final death knell of any fire.

Later that day, I had to explain my absence to Roger and in the presence of other suspicious drivers. "You should have seen the fire my brother I worked on," I told them. "The whole house burned down and the fire would have spread if we didn't put it out."

"Oh bullshit, "one of the drivers said. "I've been on the beach all afternoon and didn't see any smoke.

"Did you run into the waves again and drown your engine?" Roger asked.

"You probably went fishing again and are going to give us some bullshit about a school of blues that you caught," another driver remarked.

I denied all their concoctions and reiterated my story. It was later that evening that Roger called me into the office to tell me that two Suffolk County Policemen were there and wanted to know more about the fire. This time I was glad that Roger kept his finger on the talk button of the radio and all the drivers could eavesdrop on the conversation.

20

Celebrities

There is certainly no lack of star power out here on the island. Our history is defined, in many ways, by celebrity. Some of the most famous residents, past and present, come here for the very same reasons we do: privacy, anonymity and, yes, loads of fun.

Fire Island celebrity sightings go back into the earliest part of our history. Oscar Wilde could have been spotted near Cherry Grove in the 19th century, as well as Herman Melville in Kismet. Teddy Roosevelt even stayed at a hotel called White House at the current site of Water Island.

False

--Fire Island: The Celebrity Sandbox
by Jeffrey Salzberger with Nicole Pressly Wolf

Most days my taxi fares were of the ordinary variety, regular folks moving around the island, going from one party destination to another, mostly during evening hours. Strictly routine. I ferried the same people to the same places and sometimes at the same times every day or each weekend. Occasionally, however, there were surprises, the unexpected fares, people or circumstances that were pleasant happenstances and forever remembered.

From the office, Paul the office dispatcher radioed a call early one evening. "Pick up at Sunset Walk at Ocean Beach. Who's got it?"

Immediately I responded, "I got it Paul." I had parked on the beach only a few hundred yards from the pickup point, and no other drivers were in sight. It was the middle of the week and only three of us were working.

"10-4. I'll tell them you are already there," Paul announced.

I drove to the location and parked at the bottom of the stairs. Ten minutes went by. Soon a couple descended the stairs and headed toward my cab. The man looked middle-aged, short and balding. He wore white denim pants rolled up at the cuffs. He had his shoes in his hands. The woman was taller and had on a slip-over type dress; the kind that is worn over a bathing suit, or maybe there was nothing underneath. She appeared younger than the man did. I watched them approaching my taxi, and thought there was something strangely familiar about them. I was sure I had seen the man before.

I kept my curiosity under wraps and avoided the embarrassing and awkward moment that comes when asking, "Don't I know you from somewhere?" only to find out that I don't. Being a taxi driver wasn't a license for asking intimate questions of one's fares. Besides, I learned early that too many questions or too much idle conversation can be annoying to people, resulting in a lower tip.

The couple was quiet for the first few minutes. As we neared Cherry Grove, their destination, the woman spoke up.

"What restaurants do people usually go to here?" She asked me. I named a few, not as recommendations, but simply as names of restaurants I heard other people talk about or ones that I had seen in my wanderings around the Grove.

Then suddenly the man said to me, "We're looking for a queer one. Queers eat better than the rest of us." to which his friend replied, "Oh Mel, that's not true." Then she said to me, "Don't believe half of what he says; he's always joking around."

I had a sudden enlightenment, a light bulb kind of revelation. Instantaneously I knew from the comment he made and the raspy voice he used where I had known this man before--on television. As they left the cab, they gave me a good tip. "Thank you Ms. Bancroft, Mr. Brooks." I said.

"You're welcome," they replied. Since I addressed them by name and they did not contradict me, I was sure they were Anne Bancroft and Mel Brooks.

The first summer I worked at White Cap, I met one of my longstanding idols. The sad part is that I didn't recognize him until sometime after our encounters. In 1961, the music of Elvis Presley was still in vogue, and the popularity of the Beatles was rising. Prior to these two, only a few voices broke through to make a huge impact on popular music. One of them was the man in my taxi.

It was a freak coincidence. Over a period of a week in early June, a rather lanky middle-aged man asked me to drive him to Cherry Grove. He wasn't alone. Those with him seemed awed by his presence. They never initiated a conversation, only answered his questions. Each day following that first encounter, at just about the same time, there they were again, the lanky man along with his entourage of two or three others. I drove them to the Grove and brought them back again later in the night. They talked among themselves but occasionally addressed me, asking questions about what was happening on the island, where people liked to congregate, and how I liked driving a beach buggy. "It must be like driving in snow" was a repeated comment. This continued four days straight, and then they disappeared.

"Don't you know who that was?" one of the restaurant workers at Fire Island Pines said to me the next day, after I shared with him the episodes with the lanky man.

"I have no idea, but by the way his friends doted on him, he must be someone important," I responded.

"That was Johnny Ray."

"Who?" I asked quite innocently, not recognizing the name immediately.

"Johnny Ray. The singer, Johnny Ray. The guy who sang *Cry*, and *The Little White Cloud that Cried*."

"No shit," was about all I could muster in response. "One of my idols and nobody told me. The guy just spent four days in my cab. Why didn't you tell me who he was? I missed the chance of a life time to ask him some questions or get his autograph or tell him about myself. Oh Shit."

By 1961, the year I met him, his fame had vanished as a pop star, but it would rise once again later. Growing up in North Jersey in the 50's, not a party happened that didn't include his music, especially his hit tunes. I remember watching him on television as he dropped to his knees in despair and sang the song *Cry*, while the audience cried along with him. All my junior high friends knew that if you wanted to get a girl to make out with you, play one of Johnny Ray's songs. If I had only known that it was Johnny Ray, the famous Johnny Ray, who I ferried back and forth almost every night for a full week, I would have given a week's pay (well maybe not) just for the chance to talk with him. I could then tell my grandchildren that I once met Johnny Ray. And they would say, "Who?"

A call came in late one afternoon to the office. My brother Paul was working as dispatcher. He got on the radio and announced "Pickup at Water Island. Who's got it?" By the desperate tone of his voice, I knew he was not expecting much response from the drivers. No one replied. He asked again, "Okay folks, someone wants to be picked up at Water Island tonight at 7:00. Somebody take it, please." Still no response. There were at least three drivers in their jeeps somewhere on the beach, but none of them wanted to take a call from Water Island. Going there was to be condemned to isolation. There was virtually no business to or from Water Island unless you were a propane tank or a box of groceries.

Finally, I said, "I got it Paul. I'm headed that direction anyway for something to eat." I lived there, I felt like I was designated the official Water Island taxi dispatch.

"Okay," Paul responded. "Pick him up at 7:00 at the top of West Walk."

On my way back from a nice home cooked meal that evening, I stopped at West Walk. It was 7:00 o'clock. The fare was waiting. I noticed it was a man I saw only infrequently at Water Island. He rented a house near the west end. There was nothing unusual about his appearance. He seemed in his middle thirties, average height and weight, and with a head of tightly cropped hair. His face revealed an intense look, as if constantly perplexed and wondering about the meaning of things. He had a well-tanned body. He kept to himself most of the time except for when he attended the Fourth of July clambake sponsored by the Water Island Association. He sat by himself and only spoke when responding to someone who spoke to him first. He appeared pleasant but shy. I remember his responses that night to any question I asked was "Yes," and "Thank you," and nothing more.

As he approached the cab, I noticed how well he was dressed, unusual for folks from Water Island. He had a loose-fitting, but well ironed pastel-colored shirt open wide at the collar. His pants were the usual white denims so prevalent that year on Fire Island. Of course he had a sweater draped over his shoulders. Almost every male does the same thing with the sweater. I never saw them actually worn, only draped over the shoulders.

I greeted him, "You want to go to the Grove, right?"

"That's right, thank you" was all I got in return. Before he seated himself in the back of the taxi, he took the time to brush sand from the seat. Didn't want to get his clothes dirty, I presumed. For the duration of the trip to Cherry Grove, he didn't address me or ask any questions. I didn't press the conversation.

I stopped at the bottom of the steps that led up to Pat's Place. He asked for the fare and paid it along with a generous tip.

"I want you to pick me up right here at one," he told me. It wasn't a question so much as a demand.

"Right," I told him. "I'll be here at one." I wrote myself a note, placed it on the dashboard and as soon as I started to drive away, the note blew out the window. I didn't think I would forget, however, because I felt a slight obligation to return as instructed, since he was a neighbor from Water Island. I knew that if any other driver got him as a fare on the return trip, they would pawn him off on me anyway.

I was third in line, waiting for the "time to go home" crowd we had brought to Cherry Grove earlier that evening. It was precisely one in the morning. He came down the steps, passed by the first two cabs after not recognizing the drivers, and stopped at mine.

"You're right on time," he said.

"I told you I would be here." He got into the back seat without saying where he wanted to go. I already knew. We headed off toward Water Island. Before leaving I had explained to the other drivers that I might have a fare to Water Island. There was no protest from them.

For the next month and a half, it was always the same routine. Every Tuesday and Thursday night precisely at seven, I picked him up on the beach at Water Island and brought him down to the Grove. Again at 1:00 in the morning, I drove him home. The conversation never progressed much past "Hello," and "Good night," and "Thank you." I assumed that since he was always alone and always went to Cherry Grove, he was probably gay, but I couldn't know for sure. I had some misgivings about my assumption because he was a resident of Water Island, a tight-knitted family-oriented small community, just the opposite in attitude and behavior of Cherry Grove. Gay men didn't congregate here. We had no bars or restaurants, and no wild parties (none that I could find, and I sure looked hard), both of which I associated with the two gay communities. Because of an undertone of disdain for the gay life by the residents of Water Island, I thought it must be an uncomfortable place for gay men.

It was a Tuesday night late in August as I remember. I had parked at Water Island waiting for him to show up. When he didn't appear at the appointed time, I wondered if something might be wrong. Maybe he was sick or left the island without telling me. I waited another ten minutes when he suddenly appeared at the top of the staircase.

He yelled down to me, "I'm coming, I'm coming, Peter," It surprised me he knew my name. He had never asked, and I didn't remember volunteering it.

"Sorry I'm late. I am late aren't I?" There was a giggle in his speech and a heavy scent of alcohol on his breath. He was obviously slightly intoxicated.

On the ride to Cherry Grove, he was both animated and talkative, urged on, I assumed, by the alcohol. He initiated conversation, asking about my family, about the history of Water Island, about his feeling particularly "loose" that evening. He offered some commentary of his own, stating how he liked Water Island, liked the isolation, and wanted to buy his own house on the beach. Once he started talking, I didn't try to interrupt. I let him continue talking.

It wasn't until shortly after one thirty in the morning when he appeared for the return trip to Water Island. His inebriation was even more pronounced as he nearly stumbled down the length of the stairs leading to the beach. One of the drivers caught him before he fell face first in the sand. The driver pointed him in my direction, knowing he was going to Water Island.

He climbed in the front seat. If my assumption about his homosexuality was correct, I took this as a bad omen. Drunken gays, at this late hour, always wanted to sit in the front seat and often propositioned drivers. It wasn't because we were desirable or approachable, but rather because the gay guy was probably desperate after not finding anyone else to hook up with that night. We were a choice of last resort, with the exception of Jerry who they considered *good pickens* at any time. Although he continued to be chatty and animated for the duration of the trip, he was not aggressive or otherwise sexually offensive.

He had trouble negotiating the steps up from the beach when we arrived at Water Island. I helped him to the top where he immediately sat down.

"Are you going to be all right?" I asked. It was still a few hundred yards along a raised boardwalk to his house. I had visions of him falling off into the brambles and beach plum bushes and only found the next morning scratched up and bruised. He could blame me for not assuming liability for a drunken passenger.

"Yes, I'm fine, I think," he responded. "Why don't we sit and talk for a while. It's such a lovely night," he added. He sat down and patted the boardwalk next to him with his hand as a gesture of invitation for me to sit.

I felt a predicament unfolding. If his intentions were ultimately sexual, I wanted no part. I was adamant that wasn't going to happen. But he was also a neighbor and regular customer, and I felt it might be rude to decline. I decided to try, but remain alert and ready to bolt at the first sign of anything more than conversation.

"You can call me Edward," he said. His breath still reeked of alcohol but his speech seemed unaffected. There was small talk of little consequence until he asked directly, "What do you plan for your life. Surely you're not going to drive a taxi forever, are you?"

The comment came as an invitation. He seemed sincere in wanting to know more about me. I took his invitation also as a challenge to justify why I was driving a taxi during the summer. "No, it's just a summer job. But it's very lucrative and I need the money to finish graduate school," I told him. That comment, I felt, positioned me as someone of consequence beyond a common laborer.

"Where do you go to graduate school?" Still sensing a genuine interest on his part, I confessed that I was a first year theological student in Boston. I would probably enter the ministry at some point.

This revelation seemed to intrigue him. He asked to hear more about my decision. He listened intently while I described my "vocational journey of choice" and my field work with church youth groups. I got a bit carried away and told him more about my interest in things theological.

"I have a curiosity about things theological," he said. "Sometimes it's quite pronounced and powerful. But I haven't drawn any conclusions about God. It's a constant struggle with me." He then told me he was a writer, mostly of plays, and he often had his characters struggle with their beliefs in some higher power that they imagined had some control over their attitudes or their behavior or their ultimate destiny.

"I don't like to use theological terms though," he continued. "I feel more comfortable setting these struggles in more ordinary circumstances and having my characters explore attitudes that affect their relationships to each other. I don't like the artificial symbolism and contrived traditions of organized religion. I think they impede people's discovery of what is the truth about spiritual experience." These may not have been his exact words, but it's what I understood him to say.

This conversation happened after two o'clock in the morning on a boardwalk at Water Island with a partially intoxicated writer named Edward Albee. Only later, perhaps five more years, did I recognize the literary value of this man. Although the conversation lasted slightly less than thirty minutes, I remember it being mind-boggling. The clarity of expression he revealed so spontaneously, even after ample consumption of alcohol and the lateness of the night, was impressive. I didn't think that deeply about any subject in the past three months.

Mr. Albee grew either tired or bored with conversation. He excused himself after reassuring me that we would talk about these things again sometime. I watched him walk with a slight wobble down the boardwalk toward his house. I got back in my cab and drove the few hundred yards to my own house.

We never did talk again, at least not about anything consequential other than discussing the fare from Water Island to Cherry Grove. He continued as a regular customer for the few weeks remaining, before I had to leave to return to graduate school.

My impression of Edward Albee was of a very private person, probably one of the reasons he chose to live in the more isolated part of Fire Island. As fleeting and as brief as our conversation was that night, I appreciated the opportunity to share some relevant thoughts with him. It was one of those rare opportunities when the ordinary reveals itself as the extraordinary.

21

Fire Island Politics

The bedfellows politics made are never strange. It only seems that way to those who have not watched the courtship.

--Marcel Achard (French Playwright, 1899-1974)

Fire Island lies a mere fifty miles from Times Square, the heart of New York City. But these few miles have been sufficient to insulate it from most public displays of political opinions or radical causes. It reminded me of the Biblical exploits of Moses. When a resident crossed the shallow waters of the Great South Bay, it was as if the sea opened up, allowing the person to pass through undetected, and then immediately clamped shut again, essentially cutting him off from the rest of their world, at least for the meantime.

Rarely, if ever, did I hear an expression of political bias while on Fire Island. I don't suspect that meant residents had none. Some of the most influential political figures and pundits in America at the time spent summers on Fire Island (Geraldine Ferraro and Charles Collingwood, for instance). It just meant residents did not express political opinions while in residence on the island. They weren't prohibited, just ignored.

There is an understandable reason for this. Fire Island's reputation was as a safety valve, a place to release oneself

198

from the stresses and strains of contemporary urban culture, to let loose, to live wildly, and to forget for the moment whatever it was that needed to be forgotten, including politics, was a welcome reprieve. Its isolation made this possible. The radical change of environment, the physical separation provided by the waters of the Great South Bay, the placid waves of the ocean, the becalming effect of a car-less culture, the abandonment of movies, television, and newspapers, the necessity of having to walk most places, and, most of all, the effect of bare feet, all had the effect of numbing the political brain. Not wearing shoes for any length of time causes a person to feel more at ease, more primitive, returning them to the bare essentials. It's hard to imagine any person in bare feet and wearing spandex making major political or economic decisions. I wouldn't trust a doctor's diagnosis while she was in her bare feet and a bikini. My mother always reminded me, when she realized that I would someday become a famous preacher delivering sermons to huge congregations, "You can't fool me," she would say. "I'll still think of you in diapers and bare feet when you're in that pulpit." Bare feet and bathing suits have a way of diminishing the importance of any situation.

The residents of Fire Island avoided becoming embroiled in any controversy. It often felt like there was a convention that personal political opinions and civic causes and other things of importance that mattered to the redemption of our world be kept under wraps while in residence on the Island. I had no trouble imagining the educated, astute, and aware people I met being activists in civil rights marches, antiwar protests, or environmental causes. These highly charged emotional events of the time must have been on the minds and in the hearts of the residents, just not so when they came to Fire Island.

An exception to this axiom occurred during the summers of 1962-63. A movement had begun among some of the New York state politicians and one Robert Moses, the State Director of Parks for New York. Mr. Moses was responsible for building a bridge to the far western end of Fire Island and now wanted to construct a major thoroughfare smack down the middle of the island. Whoa, this was not about to happen. An asphalt-paved highway on Fire Island? A ribbon of concrete through Point O' Woods? The Ocean Beach Theater replaced by a road? That would be a catastrophe, so opinioned the residents.

Davis Park, Cherry Grove, Point O' Woods, and Kismet, communities whose residents hardly spoke to each other, hamlets isolated from the rest, villages that almost resented each other, suddenly became allies. They immersed themselves in a single cause--STOP THE ROAD.

The STOP THE ROAD campaign took form quickly as word spread of Mr. Moses' proposal. Even the threat of a hurricane that destroyed property and washed away whole houses didn't alarm the residents like a proposed ribbon of concrete down the middle of their beloved sand dunes. Hurricanes were inevitable. They accepted them, maybe not hoped for, but inevitable and tolerable. There was little that could be done to prevent them. But a road? That was insufferable. That was the clarion call to all residents that Fire Island was under siege and sacrificed to the goddess of development and asphalt. Residents unite. Become defenders of your property. Drive the evil road-builders back to Albany.

The real culprit and focus of the residents animosity was Mr. Moses himself. Mr. Moses had been parks director for many years. He wielded power. He was the force behind the development of Jones Beach, considered by Fire Islanders as the beach for the commonality, a place for day-trippers to congregate and scatter their soda cans, dirty diapers, snack bags, and beer bottles for someone else to clean up. It was for the urbanites that needed a respite from the city on weekends and couldn't get to Fire Island because they couldn't afford the rents for a beach cottage or the price of a ferry ticket. Fire Island afforded few amenities for the day tripper–no bath houses, no lifeguards, and no snack bars on the beach. These lacks of conveniences were omens that day-trippers weren't welcome of Fire Island.

A road meant cars, and cars meant gas stations, shopping centers, parking lots, fast food outlets, and hordes of plebeians from Queens, Brooklyn, and the Bronx. Mortal enemies. Fire Island prided itself on being an antithesis to Jones Beach.

I remember sitting on the beach on the Fourth of July, the height of the summer season, with my family. Other than a half dozen others, the beach was empty. Then Mom spoke her famous words of great compassion and empathy. "Aren't you children glad you don't have to go to Jones Beach with the crowds of people crawling over each other?" Fire Island had no hot dog stands, no carnival rides, and no ocean front boardwalk with hawkers of games and stuffed toys with which to contend. As I thought about that, with only my mother and brothers to play with, I wished I was at Jones Beach.

No cars. That was the most important non-ingredient to Fire Islanders. "We don't want Jones Beach or Atlantic City on Fire Island," became the rallying cry of the anti-road forces. The thought of cars and a roadway on the island instilled paranoia in the residents, a fear of being singled out as the only remaining obstacles to the development of the island, a development envisioned solely by Mr. Moses, so the residents thought, as nothing more than a monument to him.

The STOP THE ROAD campaign took off with a frenzy of action. Small groups formed at each of the communities and eventually joined forces with the Fire Island Voters Association (FIVA) to become more representative of the entire island. The weekly newspaper at Ocean Beach, The *Fire Island News,* became the rallying point. Their editors wrote lengthy articles and circulated them among the communities at the western end of the island. But to be successful, the campaign needed the support of the whole Island, from folks at Davis Park and Water Island and Cherry Grove and yes, even from Long Cove and Skunk Hallow. The whole island needed to be politicized if action in opposition to the road proposal would be successful.

Activists recruited White Cap taxi drivers to help spread both the news about the proposed road as well as campaign posters and literature. I volunteered my services. In my cab I carried copies of the *Fire Island News,* along with reprints of anti-road editorials, and delivered them to every restaurant, bar, post office, or meeting place imaginable on the island. I brought them to the Davis Park Casino, the Saltaire Volunteer Fire House, Flynns bar, Pats Place, and the Fire Island Pines Boatel. I placed them on the community bulletin boards of Water Island and Cherry Grove. I even posted some on the side windows of my cab until Roger "suggested" strongly that I not do this.

"Can't get any customers mad at us," he stated emphatically, "We need all the friends we got."

"But if we get a road, the taxis will be out of business." I suggested.

"If we ever do get a road, it will be long after I'm dead," he replied. That made the most sense of anything I had heard him proclaim.

Mutual confidences formed between communities of radically different personalities. I remember how Charles Collingwood, a CBS newsman and resident of one of the western family type-communities, "commissioned" my jeep to transport him to Cherry Grove and Fire Island Pines, gay communities, so that he could initiate coalitions of supporters. Unlikely support groups fashioned. Gays from Cherry Grove sat on committees with blue collar workers from Ocean Beach. Residents of tradition-bound Point O' Woods even ventured outside their gated stronghold to agree in principle with swinging singles from Davis Park. Full-time residents confided in visitors and renters, imploring them to support the ban. It proved to be a functioning coalition of the most unlikely assortment of personalities who one would suspect of having radically divergent opinions on just about every subject. On the proposed road, however, they were all in agreement and focused against it

It seemed ironic that the coalition of those opposed to a road would approach the only vehicle monopoly on the island for help. But there existed a mutual tolerance between the residents and the taxi service. The opposition was less about the few vehicles (taxis and a few small service trucks) that traversed the beach front ferrying people where they wanted to go. Residents accepted taxis along the beach as part of the ambiance of Fire Island; a tradition that maintained the style of life the residents had grown used to and wished to continue. Taxi drivers and residents had learned to coexist, each benefitting the other in a symbiotic relationship. Most importantly, from the resident's perception, taxis didn't need a road, and it was the road that caused the greatest opposition. Roads signify coming development, and development was the crucial issue.

Almost as quickly as it began, the furor over the proposed road subsided. The Governor of New York requested that Mr. Moses head up the committee for the planned World's Fair in New York, thus relieving him of responsibility for the Fire Island road project. In addition, local politicians, such as Representative Otis Pike, feeling the pressure from citizens groups, withdrew their support of the project. Almost at the same time, President Lyndon Johnson signed the National Seashore Act of 1964 which contained a provision that would eventually ban all vehicles on National Seashore property.

The short-lived coalitions that had formed to fight the roads disbanded. There was to be no road and by the beginning of the next summer, it was a completely dead issue. There were celebrations for the victory, but also a certain amount of lamenting for the good old days with its limited beach traffic and the availability for residents to patronize other communities. The park service banned vehicles in some parts of the island almost immediately, in others over a period of time. Although White Cap taxis continued to provide limited service into the early 70's, the National Seashore act spelled an end to the service. Fire Island remained road less.